AF343538

CONFESSIONS OF A FORGER
The hidden face of the art market

Éric Piedoie Le Tiec

CONFESSIONS OF A FORGER
The hidden face of the art market

Max Milo

Max Milo, Paris, 2022
www.maxmilo.com
ISBN : 978-2-315-00066-0

To Caesar

To all the great artists who advance ideas

Contradiction YES
Contradiction NO
Yvan Alechinsky

Foreword

Only the dream transformed into reality is a Grail. To create, to understand others, artists, human beings. I am an analytical contemplative who only knows how to use his eye and, a little, his defragmented brain. Thinking that it is better to do nothing with one's life than to miss it, I am interested in that of others, of creators, of plastic artists, of artists who have amazed me by their existence and by the creative force they have conveyed throughout the fabulous modern era in plastic art.

I tried to understand them, to penetrate their fucking history, their life in their deepest intimacy, to analyze the mysteries of these great masters who have, through their work, had an impact on the evolution of thought. I went so far as to dissect them, to feel them, to hate them, to love them, to remake them, and even to reinvent them without deceiving them. Certainly, deep down, feeling that they have been understood, they would have approved.

I deeply believe that art is a lie that makes us understand the truth. Forgeries have swarmed in history, and especially in art, in the last fifty years. In the 1960s, Fernand Legros was the instigator of this chaos. This grandiloquent and flamboyant character sold whole lots of forgeries of Picasso, Matisse, Chagall, Marquet, Utrillo to rich Americans, with the complicity of the Parisian galleries Pétridès. Helmyr de Hory, the other great forger of the 20th century, specialized in painting in the manner of Modigliani and Picasso, with the tip of his charcoal and his brush... and considerably enriched the production of the greatest!

Among the cases that still fascinate amateurs, we could mention the adventure of Geert Jansen and Ellen Van Baren, a Dutch couple arrested in 2001 for producing six thousand modern lithographs. Fake, of course. Guy Ribes, too, has produced Matisse, Renoir, Modigliani, Chagall, and Picasso. And what can we say about Han Van Meegeren, who was so fascinated by the golden age of the Dutch and in particular Vermeer that the greatest experts fell into his trap? Today, his works can be found in museums. David Stein, on the other hand, specializes in Picassos, Matisses, Klee and other Chagalls - it was the latter who, in 1966, uncovered the trick - as well as Andy Warhol's fake *Superman*.

Fakes are everywhere in art: in museums, exhibition halls, galleries, and this for a simple reason: these masterpieces are made with the complicity of the masters themselves (sometimes), of the artists' families when they are dead (very often), of experts and gallery owners from all over the world (all the time). Everyone wins.

The forger, first of all. The work of an unknown is worth nothing; the same work, signed by a master, is worth a fortune. The artist forger thus amasses colossal sums of money, as much as a drug trafficker.

The artist also wins. Without being obliged to create, the famous painter can monetize his signature with forgers and speculators. Dalí, Picasso and many others have understood this!

Finally, the rightful claimants gain. Indeed, when a master dies, the family and his entourage have a stock problem. When all the masterpieces have been sold, it is in their financial interest to authenticate new works, especially since the flow of rich amateurs who want to invest in art does not dry up. These last fifty years have coincided with the overbidding of the quotation of many artists. A real hunt for fakes!

For my part, I have been making forgeries for forty years, with the complicity of the artists, their mistresses, their families, their friends, the experts and the gallery owners, in an atmosphere of sex, drugs and creation. I found my masterpieces in exhibitions, Christie's and Sotheby's catalogs, in the great galleries of the United States, London, Japan, Korea and the Rue de Seine... An orgy!

In 2001, at the time of the César scandal, the press presented me as the emperor of forgery. *Le Figaro* was astonished that, in spite of my immoderate love of art, in spite of my talent, in spite of my genius, I had never thought of rubbing shoulders with Monet or Rembrandt, nor with Rodin or Maillol. I answer that I prefer to play with contemporary artists. Monet is not a period that interests me. Too far from me and my idea of art. For Rembrandt, there is already a very famous forger who makes a lot of them. Same thing for Van Gogh. For the old painters, the cases of forgery have multiplied and have given rise to resounding trials concerning Rodin, Maillol, Claudel and Bourdelle. Guy Hains had hundreds of sculptures made in his foundry in Luxeuil-les-Bains that were prized on the international market.

I have in my collection a beautiful Monet (real), a small Rembrandt and a fake Rodin, accumulated during my years of creative madness. This Rodin, about thirty centimeters, in bronze with a green patina, issued and recognized as authentic, appeared during the German occupation in Paris, when the Nazis had taken over the ministries and museums. A Nazi took a particular interest in Rodin and took the mold of *The Eternal Adoration*, which depicts a naked man and woman ready to make love. This bronze was cast in a foundry in the Lyon area. Only three copies were made by the founder, whose personal stamp is stamped on the work, along with Rodin's signature. The mold was real, it came from the Rodin Museum. I acquired my sculpture from a studio technician who had been Claude François' musical arranger and, his glory days being far behind him, found himself obliged to resell his collection. *Through* an intermediary, he thus enriched me with a very beautiful mobile by Calder from the 1940s and this fake Rodin.

I was never a *fan of* Rodin, but seeing this object on my desk all the time, I found myself liking it. This fake was valued at two and a half million dollars. Later, I was contacted by a very famous actor who collected works by Claudel, Rodin and Picasso, and had even played the role of Rodin in the movies. In short, Gérard Depardieu wanted to buy my fake. I didn't sell it to him. You don't sell what you like!

1. Saint-Paul-de-Vence:
Calder, Ben and César [1970]

As a teenager, I was fortunate to live in an enclave inhabited by many painters, musicians and filmmakers from around the world. In this place, we were taught a philosophy of life that immediately interested me. Creation was a common place for everyone; the words "freedom", "love", "libertinage", "madness", "non-action" were the primary values of Tourrettes-sur-Loup. As much for the history of art as for geography, this village has been associated on the one hand with Vence, the town where Matisse, Dubuffet, Ernst worked; and on the other hand, further down the road with Saint-Paul, where these great artists found refuge to satisfy their desires for libertinage and work.

Saint-Paul has seen Soutine and Modigliani come and go, but also old-timers like Renoir, who lived not far from there, on the heights of Cagnes-sur-Mer. Calder and Miró have also left works on the city's hunting list, which can be seen today at the Maeght Foundation. Arman had his home-studio there. Not far from there, César filled the Colombe d'Or with magnificent pieces that can be seen between Picasso cubists, Miró anthologies, Delaunay, Léger and many others. Giacometti and Chagall came to work here. They are now resting in the small cemetery of Saint-Paul.

As far as I was concerned, I was fifteen years old and I was fascinated by so much concentrated energy. Not being able to travel, I had the urge to visit with friends the magnificent exhibitions offered by the Côte d'Azur galleries, the openings and *happenings* of Ben or the Fluxus movement. One of my friends, a painter and visual artist, told me that he had attended a *happening* by Yoko Ono. She was part of this Fluxus group of thought. He described the *show to* me in detail. She was alone on a stage, in a kind of small improvised theater; she was dressed in a black dress and moved without a word on this stage.

At the entrance, scissors were handed out to all spectator-actors, so that everyone could cut out a piece of the dress. When Yoko Ono came down from her promontory and moved among the audience, everyone had to cut the dress in order to make the performer naked. It was fascinating to see that some people were shy and only cut a small piece, while others were greedy and tore off whole sections. Yoko was naked very quickly. It was a tribute to Marcel Duchamp and his *Bride Stripped Bare by her Bachelors, even.*

Impressed by the story, I imagined this performance and have not forgotten it. I wish I could have been there. Yoko Ono repeated this *happening* in New York some time later, but I could not be there. I had no idea that art could be just an ephemeral action; for me it required brushes, pencils, a subject, canvas and colors.

I spent my nights at the homes of all these artists who drowned in drugs and alcohol all the reasons they had to exist. With my friends, we would crash at Billy Wyman's place in the hills of Vence. There was often a known fauna of musicians, Mick Jagger, groupies, and even Murray Head who never supported Vence and told me one day:

- It's a dead city, full of assholes. I've been at Billy's for a year now, and while it looks really *cool*, I'm bored. You want a rail? I'll introduce you to my girlfriends, it's gonna be a hot night.

Around Mick, beaming, his *girlfriends* were untouchable. All over the place, a lot of *people* were out of their minds, completely out of control, perched high, high. My buddies and I got into the spirit of things: chicks, champagne and other drugs. We danced like crazy until the next day when, exhausted by the orgy, we left alone, keeping once again the ether of our debauchery in memory. That was my life. This multiculture forced me to flutter around in a whirlpool of delirious people gravitating around hallucinated geniuses... I learned lessons of limitless freedom, love and sex. It was the 1970s.

In the vernissages, I could see from afar characters like Calder, very simple but impressive of corpulence and surrounded by rare living deities of the modern era. He was waving his hand as if he was greeting the guests around, charmed to be recognized by the ogre-child. In reality, he was simply suffering from Parkinson's disease and was trembling, feverish, constantly vibrating, just like his mobile sculptures. The little snobs were flattered because, except for me, no one knew about it.

It was in private that I was able to approach this monster, thanks to the parents of my friends who knew him. This brilliant man behaved like a child in wonder who is amused by life. He made his own existence a theater, whose actors were small wire sculptures, each representing a character and circus animals. Of this, I only know the films from the 1940s, when his audience was a tiny group of Surrealist, Dadaist and Cubist artists who were as unknown as he was at the time. Having had the good fortune to be around lithographers and ceramists who worked for him, all of whom were affiliated with the Maeght structure, I was able to penetrate his creative space better than by talking to him. Calder did not express

---

1. SAINT-PAUL-DE-VENCE: CALDER, BEN AND CÉSAR [1970]

himself much and was too impressive for me to have the courage to ask him questions. So I went through his collaborators, if I may call them that, who were master engravers and ceramists.

On Calder's advice, his assistants executed in the workshops of the Maeght Foundation the techniques that the master did not master. Calder delegated his creations to specialists. They were his regular executors but also those of certain artists, such as Miró or others: these geniuses did not master the craft essential to many of their works. Calder knew "only" how to twist metal, paint it and balance it so that, once finished, the sculpture was entirely the plaything of the wind, the elements, space, and its movement became free.

In his preparatory gouaches, I see only spirals, rounds of bright colors, orange, yellow, red - colors full of life, like him. I soon learned that when the amount of work becomes important, even for a monster of solidity, there are techniques with which only specialists can translate the imagination and wishes of the artist himself. They are in a way the technical extensions of his thought, but will never be, even in osmosis at the moment of the common result, the artist himself. I understood that they could bring me important elements on the arcane of the master's thought. By staying close to these specialists, I was able to better understand these exceptional beings.

I also understood that the artist could, for many reasons, imagine a concept and have it executed by others, to whom he would explain its purpose. I sensed that the association between thoughts, canvases, colors and brushes was obsolete. In the future, creation would be stripped of techniques. I discovered this even more when I was "in class". In fact, I spent most of my time in the darkness of the cinematheque's projection room, where films on the lives of Miró, Chagall, Giacometti or Braque were constantly shown. Watching them work in their private studios was enough to get me excited. I then started to deconstruct their behavior to better know them and, *in fine,* to understand them. The art of inventing cannot be reduced to purely mechanical processes, it is the result of a philosophical and creative approach.

On a Sunday afternoon, as a tourist, how can one *feel* a Giacometti, when facing his skinny, lanky, agonizing sculpture, if one does not somehow penetrate the sculptor's private life through books and films? What can one feel without knowing that, all his life, the artist has only reproduced his own image of starvation? Today, this image of suffering is proposed and sold, declined in postcards in a strictly lucrative goal whereas, he either, never drew from his art a pecuniary consecration: at the end of his life, he was salaried, fed and lodged by the Maeght foundation.

My grandfather, a painter and architect, gave me a camera and all the accessories I needed to capture moments of life by fixing them forever. That Nikon and I became inseparable. It served as an intermediary between my ideas, my desire to catch privileged moments without needing to get too close to the subjects, the people and the artists. It served me as a passport to unlock the sacrosanct mysteries of those who made up the art world, the places where works were made, the studios of Arman in Vence, Ben in Nice, César in Roquefort-les-Pins. I photographed the *happenings* of Pinoncelli. I was able to capture the emotion, to steal the memory of the time, I who did not know how to hold a pencil, a charcoal or anything that would have allowed me to express myself otherwise.

My grandfather had reminded me that, nine centuries earlier, our oldest known ancestor, Hugues Piedoie, a close friend of Saint Louis, was also an architect and painter. Saint Louis, the man who dispensed justice under his oak tree, commissioned him around 1250 to build the parish church of Saint-Martin in Longjumeau, in the Essonne region, contemporary with the construction of Notre-Dame de Paris. This church, dedicated to Bishop Martin of Tours,

---

1. Saint-Paul-de-Vence: Calder, Ben and César [1970]

was destroyed and then rebuilt during the wars. My grandfather Hugues Piedoie, therefore, was far from imagining that, nine centuries later, I would be a painter and forger. If I could go back in time, I would ask him to put in a good word for me so that I could get out *clean* of the numerous legal cases that have marked my life and that I could have done without!

2. The Shadow of a Genius:
Klein, Saint Phalle and Raysse
[1973]

After the *hippie* high school in Vence, I decided to take the entrance exam for the Arts Déco in Nice. During several months of preparation, I wander from museum to gallery, from library to private classes of drawing and color study. At the end of the day, I failed because I was too academic and not open enough. In fact, I didn't have the necessary mastery to enter this high place of education from which almost all the great visual artists and theorists of the time emerged. Nice is nevertheless the cradle, among others, of Yves Klein, the inventor of the ultramarine blue monochrome; of Arman, the accumulator of heterogeneous objects, the destroyer fixing his anger in resin and making it eternal; of César, the greatest of all, inventor of the recycling of consumer objects into compressions/art pieces; Niki de Saint Phalle who, after her rifle shots on canvas, invented *La Femme,* which she named *La Hon,* femme étalon, in ultra-colored resin representing a thirty-meter long, six-ton colossus that she defined as the biggest whore in the world; Martial and France Raysse, who honored love by inlaying neon lights in their canvases that can be seen in the city's Museum of Modern Art! All of them came from or were close to the Arts déco of Nice.

I fall back on the Villa Thiole, an elitist competition preparation school, where I try to understand the basics of fabrication and plastic expression. I am the worst student. My line is heavy; exaggerated is my vision of proportions in volume. Very quickly, these courses make me singularly drunk, but I must learn at all costs or, at least, grasp by guessing. No question of remaining on the sidelines without knowing anything, at the risk of never catching this elusive thing that my teachers-artists try until the overdose to inculcate me. Except that I am blocked, hermetic, stuck. When I draw, the teachers throw away my easel and take back my charcoal to finish or redo my exercise themselves: alone, I would never have been able to finish my shit. I feel an enormous frustration there; and this shame remains in me as long as, by dint of work, I do not arrive at a *minimum of* a small result.

At the Villa Thiole, the monster of color teaching is called Huguenin. He is a corpulent character, about sixty years old, a failed painter who has remained on the fringe of the art world. A former student of Fernand Léger, during the painter's post-American period, he was one of his executors, a sort of worker helping the master to assemble his frames, take over sketches or finish what the artist asked him to do for him.

I realize that most of the great artists of this century have had executors to help them realize their projects. Nothing new, however: since Raphael, the history of art has been a group effort. Direction, choice of colors and materials, signature, glory and fortune for the artist; execution and a worker's salary for the little hands. Huguenin could not bear to live in the shadow of a genius because he was never recognized as an artist. So he ended his life trying to train those who might be what he had failed to be. He did his best to teach his pupils the meaning, the balance and the value of colors, to give us to see what only a trained eye can discern, to teach us to dissect colors and to decompose them before mixing them on the palette and to arrive at a transposition as accurate as personal of the observation.

The colors that we don't see, I end up seeing them by dint of concentration until exhaustion. I separate them and put them back in their place on the canvas. I learn that, placed on a table of dark sienna color, a pot captures purple, blue, red or pink reflections; and it is these reflections that I must paint. The edge of the table on which this pot is placed appears to me with green reflections, even apple green sometimes. By dint of self-denial, tears, irritation and renunciation, I succeed in acquiring a new vision; it took me a year of intense training. I also understand that, in order to work as a team, it is essential to magnetize one's performers to make them understand the concepts of the works to be realized. Then, these executors become clones of the artist - I will remember this when, like an assistant following the tacit instructions of a genius, I will execute forgeries of certain masters.

Huguenin would never experience this liberation. The repression of his own art led him, like most of the teachers at the Villa, to neurosis. The teachers and I don't function in the same way, which explains why they treat me, rightly or wrongly, as a moron who can't grasp the heart of the art that they themselves are convinced they have grasped. And I, for my part, think that Huguenin is stupid to have missed his destiny. He had everything to be a mad forger; he was the very heart of Fernand Léger; but his *ego* was too strong. His resentment and honesty trapped him in frustration until his death. What a waste!

3. My hunting paintings: Legros, Léger and Chagall [1976]

At Villa Thiole, the magical life of Fernand Legros inspires me. During the 1960s, this artist forger had the whole world in his pocket - experts, rightful owners, dealers and painters' widows. Reading his masterpiece, *Tableaux de chasse ou la vie extraordinaire de Fernand Legros*, I begin to dream of a free, libertine and offbeat life, where a certain magic can change a dull existence into a bouquet of lights.

One morning, in need of money, I consulted some auction catalogs while drinking a tea, and I decided to get busy. Digging through my drawing boxes, recovering a few sheets of Canson paper, I soak these too white sheets in my Earl Grey. Yellowing as if it had been exposed to the sun for too long, the sheet ages, when dried, by about forty years! Grabbing a pencil, I summarily execute a drawing found in a Dufy catalog: it is a scene of carriages, with horses and ladies in crinolines, sketched in the Jardin Albert-Ier in Nice (Raoul Dufy's favorite subject in the 1940s). I find the drawing nice; so I decide to go and offer it on the market of second-hand dealers, antique dealers and merchants of infamous crusts which is held in the Old Nice, cours Saleya. After two or three refusals, I arouse the interest of a peddler for this "masterly" work, resulting from a morning lamentation. I immediately cashed in the equivalent of 900 €. I laugh, and the dealer laughs too, convinced that he has just made a good deal. He asks me if I have other family works to give him. I let him think that I did, thus arousing his interest in my collection, which is certainly non-existent but which is just waiting for some personal efforts to be made to expand it.

After my classes, I begin, awkwardly, to sketch sketches, drawings, compositions in the manner of Fernand Léger. I go to the Fernand-Léger national museum in Biot. There, I study the different periods of his work. I analyze the papers, the gouache colors and the inks used by the artist. I preciously note my observations, especially those related to the American period. I spend hours between the museum rooms and the library, rich in information. I take photos that I can use to make new studies on paper with ink and gouache, works that I intend to invent and realize in the intellectual logic of Léger transmitted by Huguenin.

Later, by frequenting very important collectors, I would learn that, when she became a widow, Nadia Léger continued to create works by her husband. The collectors explained to me that only works authenticated during the master's lifetime, provided they were major works, were of interest to them; the others were tainted by suspicion. Mine are not important works, barely studies on paper, done in graphite, ink and gouache. They are no less respectful of the spirit of the master; I therefore date them before his death, sign them with his name, and sell them without a second thought to my little merchants on the Cours Saleya. After that, I set about creating works in Chagall's wash. To achieve this, I analyze already finished works, I go back to the framework of the preliminary drawing, and I recompose, in another balance, a new sketch in 40x60 cm. Out of my six attempts, four seem worthy of being preserved. I contact a gallery in Monaco which also lends money in exchange for the deposit of jewelry or works of art. The gallery and its director took me for a high-spending heir, squandering his family's assets. This saves me from having to expose myself to the unnecessary risks of direct sales and pressing questions. The gallery offers me the equivalent of a few hundred euros per work, and the possibility of getting them back within a year... with an interest rate!

My work in Miró's mixed media - gouaches, charcoal, Indian ink and graphite - is really not great: I'm ashamed of it today! But I'm still learning and my student purse is filling up with ease. This allows me to party, pay for my coke rails and buy my first Beetle convertible.

4. The meeting:
Warhol, Lichtenstein and Mandrake
the magician [1979]

During this period of learning, I jumped on the art train without a ticket. With my friends of promotion, we are overboosted by chemistry and shot with heroin. We are invited to all the crazy parties. One of the most memorable is Andy Warhol's opening at the Hotel de Paris in Monaco: between the barriers that hold back an uninvited public and the valets who are hallucinating in front of our green crests and our *look*, we're a mess in Monaco. Surrounded by Ferraris, Bentleys and other ultra-luxury cars, my Beetle Convertible is picked up by the valet. We head straight for Warhol. He is in a corner of the showroom in a blazer and a blonde wig. He stands still, hands behind his back like a diva, responding to a wall of people standing more than a meter away from him. Only his secretary translates, photographs and records the event.

During the tour, we go back and forth to the bar. A lot. I spot Caesar in a hallway near the reception. Clearly intimidated by the *pop art* star, he keeps himself busy by punching a stack of *Interview* magazine to sign autographs for punk midget girls in Chanel. Warhol was unaware that Caesar was unknown in the United States.

A few grams of alcohol later, my buddies and I are taken in picture without our knowledge by the secretary of the *star*, who invites us to stay for dinner under the glass roof with 300 privileged people. I decline the invitation: we want to leave to continue the party elsewhere, in Nice, with friends. When the secretary insists, arguing that Warhol has changed the composition of his table to include us - there are four of us - I give in; and we do what we are invited to do: plant our existentialist scandals by emptying the bottles of Chablis, then recommend other bottles. Warhol doesn't move. He is content to observe the incessant ballet of the waiters.

We are the darlings and pariahs of the evening. The dishes follow one another, nobody touches them but us! The vampire Warhol is watching us. We are his attraction. He does not speak, addressing only his secretary and remaining, as usual, at the stage of the deeply superficial and futile. The secretary serves as a relay interpreter and gauges us: who are we? what are we doing? *No answer!* It is enough to observe us to understand. This is the sport that most of the dinner guests are playing, their eyes riveted on our table. I imagine the conversations...

In reality, this dinner - where I don't see Caesar - is only a *happening* discreetly directed by the masterful vampire Andy. Everything is calculated. Warhol hates Monaco and its fauna. To hold on, he needs *destroyed* existential *fun*, like his work. We are his willing toys. The secretary, taut as a bow, translates in bursts the questions that Warhol asks us. The artist is not looking for a dialogue, but he wants to know who are these punks with green, red, blue, white Perfecto, diaphanous and without any doubt completely stoned? No dialogue of the deaf. Our presence has an advantage for him: it positions him as an overhanging deity, half-amused, half-misunderstanding. The frustrated looks of the Monegasque pseudo-intelligence amuse him. It's his way of sending these snobs away from him. He is the MC and plays with us, for example by letting his wine drip like blood on the corner of his lips. Does he think he is in osmosis with us? Not sure.

Via his secretary, he asks me if I own at least one of his works. I answer him:

- No, not one, several. Silkscreens on canvas, one of which represents four Marilyn Monroe of different colors, four *Campbell's Soup Cans* also silkscreened on four separate canvases, and a gloomy *Electric Chair* on canvas.

What I don't specify? A tiny detail: these are my first tests made a few days before. I probably bluffed him, but he's careful not to show it!

- I don't like Monaco," Andy grumbles. I'm bored there. In the gardens and on these tables, I wish there were only artificial flowers.

The pope of *pop art* is surrounded by *ultra light* beings, but his logic of "deeply superficial" is not light!

The secretary asks us if we would agree to finish the evening in Andy's suite. We accept and we find ourselves, Andy, his secretary and us, to make flow with Louis Xlll cognac and Cristal Roederer champagne. Finally, we don't have to hide anymore to sniff! A tape of what Andy filmed in sixteen years at the Factory, on the theme of the "Thirteen most beautiful women in the world", is played on a loop: a fixed shot of each face for long minutes, women with frozen expressions; only a few mouth movements, eyelash beats, discreet breaths or movements of the nerves of the face animated them. Disturbing, no sound, no action. Vampire Andy!

The master confides to us - I already suspected - that he is obsessed with Picasso. Picasso is the greatest artist in this *bloody story of art* and yet one of the most prolific. I agree with Andy. I tell him that I also have several Picassos hanging on my walls.

These are, of course, fakes. From real Picassos, authenticated studies on paper, indisputable of truth and mastery, I made others in graphite and gouache, on subjects such as *The Painter and his Model, Heads of Fauns,* as well as nudes of very fat women, attempts at cubist composition... All of this makes up about fifteen interpretations of the master, not really successful, still in their infancy, but which I signed "Picasso" and dated from his lifetime. I hid these works in my drawing box, in the middle of my own studies, those I did at the Arts Déco. By making these drawings and gouaches, I understand Picasso more, the speed of his strokes, the accuracy of his compositions. I understand him more intimately than a course given by the best art teacher would have revealed to me. I have no intention of selling them. It is only a work of analysis, personal and imperfect.

Without this subtitle, the vampire seems once again disconcerted. He blurts out:

- For an artist like me, the most important thing is to produce without rest, without stopping. That's what I do in my Factory in New York, my factory for creating art.

The introverted genius would finally open up to us? Then I jumped in and told him, sincerely, that he was the only one who deserved the name of master, in the New York scene, even in the face of colossi like Pollock, Lichtenstein, Jasper Johns and Wesselmann. I would add that he seems to me very close to the New Realism of Nice, to César, Arman and Klein. In my opinion, these three dig a similar path by relentlessly questioning consumer society. New realism and *pop art* evolve in parallel, simultaneously, barely separated by the distance between New York and Nice. I take advantage of this to slip in the fact that I have a very beautiful work by Roy Lichtenstein, an enlarged comic strip image silk-screened on canvas, but also black and white photos of Roy working, which the artist has signed and autographed for me; and, thrown in, I amuse myself by asking him:

- Why do you think Lichtenstein never reproduced in large format the hero of my favorite comic strip, Mandrake, the magician with his cape, his wand, his top hat, always accompanied by his eunuch bodyguard, wearing a ring in his ear?

Andy looks at me and nods off. He has talked too much, listened too much...

He is an icon, the pope of our time. He took on the best subjects of his time. He invented popular art. He understood everything!

Thanks to the Polaroid of my dismantled face, taken by his secretary during the dinner, I will have, two years later, my face realized on a silk-screened canvas of 120x120 cm, polychrome square, black background. Signed ! I installed it next to my other works of the brilliant *pop artist*. These works, I will never put them on sale, rather to die. They materialize the fleeting moments of an improbable night, now printed in detail in my memory...

5. The concept: Arman, Manzoni and Fontana [1982]

For the artist, the fraud does not consist in resembling his legend: it consists in trying to correspond to the fantasies of the customers, the collectors, the gallery owners, the dealers; it consists in going in the direction of the criticisms that the public swallows without understanding anything and by paying very expensive. What must be grasped is the concept of the master, the divine part of his creation.

In the work of Arman, the great guru of New Realism, the concept jumps out at you, subjugates you. One day, an architect, a professor of urban planning at the Arts Déco de Nice, invited me to visit Arman in his property in Vence. Arman wanted to transform his studio and, to do so, to take pictures. It is a traditional-looking house, located on the heights of Vence, with a wonderful view of the sea and the surrounding area. Its originality: inside, a staircase gives access to two wooden dodecahedrons, nested one in the other. In one, there is the artist's room; in the other, his reflection room. Arman's goal is to destroy these spaces to enlarge his living and working spaces. He offers me to recover them. Not having a place to install them, I decline the offer.

My architect-urbanist friend introduces me. The master barely glances at me. I take the opportunity to slip away and visit the surroundings of the property, in order to take pictures of just about everything that looks interesting. The strangest thing is that, to get to the front door of this house, you have to cross a sloping garden and zigzag between hundreds of pianos laid out in any manner. There are grand pianos and uprights, thrown like corpses in a cemetery grave. Some instruments have been lying for years, slumped on themselves, scattered on the ground without any human intervention - only the sun, the rain and the wind have destroyed these objects. While some of the more recent instruments are still standing, others are nothing more than a line of black and white keys, like teeth stuck in a skull. Some pianos lean against each other as if to avoid falling and try to stay alive as long as possible. Of this dereliction, only time and weather are guilty; and only Arman is witness, listener and conductor of a music of which he perceives, at best, only the sporadic cracking of the wood and the clacking of the rusty strings giving way from time to time.

Around his pool, behind a bush, I also discover, hallucinated, hundreds of telephones placed on the ground. On the lawn, old black bakelite communication tools, from almost all eras, planted for life for nothing, without hope of resonating one day to transmit some message. Not being connected to any network, they are the tools of an ultra-private communication - a divine logorrhea without a fixed interlocutor, an infinite question asked to the dead and by them, a suspension of certainty offered to the imaginary. These unconnected *dead phones* certainly communicate in encrypted form with an afterlife. No bugging possible! I imagine myself bathing and watching this gathering of phones while waiting for one of them to start ringing for me. I took a picture of this surreal scene and have contemplated this image often since. The fact that Arman ignores me opens me, without the need for the artist to subtitle his work, to the personal, intuitive, profound discovery of his concept. The master opens a door to his mind, his vision of things, and lets my fantasies roll in his aesthetic sauce.

I got even closer to art and its concepts when I was bitten by the Italian *arte povera*, especially by Manzoni's work from the 1960s. This artist is most famous for keeping samples of his own shit in sealed cans labeled: *Merda d'artista*. The cans were limited editions, therefore numbered and sold in galleries. To this day, only a few museums keep an official record of them. With this provocation, which was much more than a provocation, art reached an organic stripping. Manzoni proclaimed and proved that everything was art. Even shit could, in a conceptual way, become a museum work. How many of us have dreamed - we must dare to use this word - about what those opaque boxes really contained! It happened that, in public, some profaners deflowered one of them... and discovered another box, smaller, that they did not dare to profane. The truth is that we should never try to demystify concepts. Let's keep them for what they are: supports for the imagination.

Like shit, the blood of an artist, projected on canvas, can become *body art*. It comes out of the artist's own guts, without intermediaries such as brushes, tubes of colors, pigments mediums in red colored powder. The blood of the artist - not always *clean* - and nothing else! We played with it. We loaded syringes of our blood, projected them on large white canvases, in an anarchic, undirected way, in balanced compositions or not. Our *bloods were* all red in color, but of different intensity. Even the nobles projected a "beggar" red blood, while we were hoping to see *blue blood*... Disappointment, but great result anyway! The living blood, projected en masse by all the members of the Body'Blood-Artist group, continued to light up this white canvas brightly and then, before our eyes, transformed into brown sprays and spots. With bright red blood, we would make a canvas whose *blood* colors would fix, dying and drying, first in brown, then in black, cracking and decomposing, fixing itself forever on the virginal canvas. Of this living art destroying itself, we were creators and spectators. It announced the mutation of our globules and our own end. I was thinking of the death of our *blood:* it predicted a very *dark* end!

I also felt the need to preserve the master's imagination when I tried my hand at Fontana. His fanaticism, his sensuality, his strength touched me on all levels. His red and green monochromes on canvas, in which he lacerates the painted canvas with a razor stroke, vertically or obliquely. These two or three slashes allow the canvas to open slightly inward, like a woman's sex, hemming in on the sides like lips. At the back of the canvas, to close the laceration, Fontana lays black tarlatan, like an opaque bridal tulle, forming a kind of untouchable hymen as works of art. By making one myself, I want to feel the emotion that Fontana must have experienced when he created his works.

To achieve this, I had stretchers made that were similar to his. I used the same canvas as his - ultra fine linen - and the same colors. However, I lacerated the support as I wished, without copying the master, letting my imagination take over. My lacerations infused me with Fontana's eroticism and sensitivity; I executed them with, I believe, just as much pleasure. I imagined what he could get out of lacerating his monochromes with a razor. I was happy with the result. I was reaching what I wanted. To understand what the artists live at the moment of the creation of the work and to live it in my own way: this is my dream. Being a spectator is not my thing. I want to know everything, to know everything, to understand everything. In this case, I was happy with the result. I even wrote the title *Conzietto spazialle on the* back of the canvas, as the artist himself did. I signed "Fontana" and dated my creations to the same period as his. I didn't copy, I took the idea and did what I wanted with it.

The Fontana's are highly rated on the art market, so I manage to sell the products of my inspiration for the equivalent of 100 000 €. I feel like I am avenging the man who, in the 1960s in Italy, sold his creations for almost nothing. I am surprised that I am ordered again, and that I am offered to buy them in lots of 50 to 100 paintings. Of course, the prices become wholesale prices, which forces me to sell Fontana's art and to sell it off. I accepted once, to recover financially, but no more: this betrayal, in contradiction with my respect for the work, already seemed unworthy. Later, I learned that there was a foundation to protect the artist's rights, especially his rating. Logically, the results of the sale of the works fall into the hands of the rightful owners, him being dead... At the time, I don't want to believe that people who are supposed to be experts are unable to differentiate between the real and the fake. It will take me some time to admit that history and the art business are definitely two very different things.

I have not had any backlash from my fake Fontanas. I saw them again in international fairs, in galleries, at the FIAC, in Basel, in Miami. What a joy, always renewed, to see my works mixed with those of the master!

6. Fulton Street: Matisse, Picasso and Cézanne [1983]

My work as a forger takes shape. It takes a frankly *borderline* step during a *trashy* party, when I meet Richard Fulton. I was not aware at the time that this guy was going to become an active accomplice in my libertine life, in violent *happenings* and debauched parties, artistically organized and filmed. His great-grandfathers melted steel into railroad tracks in the United States. Richard inherited the shares of this heavy industry, as well as one of the largest collections of modern and ancient art, and he melted them into *coke* rails. Always accompanied by Jaimie, his friend-amant-trav'-trash-thaï, he lives between New York - he has a monstrous pied-à-terre on Park Avenue that he almost never occupies - and the Flossane estate, a large mansion in front of the village of Saint-Paul. Very quickly, this paradisiacal place shelters our evenings high, debauchery, sex, perversion, dope and white ladies for killing madness.

While sniffing our lifelines, we devise a strategy to squander the *Fulton Family*'s fabulous modern art collection. Her *sweet* mother having blocked an ultra-consistent inheritance because of her expensive and *destroyed* side, we decide, as a first step, to make an inventory of the major modern works - Chagall, Picasso, Albert Giacometti, Max Ernst and more - that invaded the picture rails of the Flossane estate in Saint Paul and the New York apartment on Park Avenue. We substitute clones for the real, important works. It is up to me to make the copies.

We leave for the 800 m² *flat* in the American Gardens Bulding, on Park Avenue, which only ghosts inhabit, leaving the custody of the Flossane estate to Jaimie. No regrets: anyway, he couldn't show up at New York customs without being scanned from head to toe and body searched. Jaimie doesn't travel without half of the *Vidal* toxicology table in his luggage. The risk of Richard, Jaimie and I being stuck in customs or more is too great. The stakes lead us to be cautious. Richard and I must concentrate on: the Orientalist Matisse; the Cubist Picassos; the *Portrait of Coco as a Child* by Renoir in Cagnes-sur-Mer - the master's high period, a work listed in the Daulte catalog; a drawing by Cézanne, in this case a watercolor and graphite study of a *Montagne Sainte-Victoire*. That's it! The Fultons' collection was acquired by their forebears directly from the artists themselves, for certain masterpieces, as well as through dealers such as Vollard and Khanweiler. All of these rare works are of excellent provenance, with unquestionable authentications. Deceased, grand-papy-chemin de fer will not die. It is time to enjoy it.

To help me make the clone-copies, I brought from Vienna a relation of the Art Deco school in Nice, a very talented forger. Helmut specialized in the second half of the 19th century until the 1970s. He arrives at the Park Avenue *flat* with a barda of pigment powders, old canvases of which he has kept only the fabric, scraping the scabs that covered them, with the frames of the time, with his oils made according to the recipes of the time, as well as with his brushes and his mastery of a great professional of forgery. We need a month of delirium and intense work to be as close as possible to the works we clone. We free ourselves from the pressure of our work with explosive nights in the trendy places of New York, where we gorge ourselves with sex, alcohol and dope. The music penetrates us.

When I can, I visit trendy museums and galleries, especially those of Mary Boone and Leo Castelli, with whom I am in contact. I hone my knowledge of avant-garde art by visiting the new gallery shows on Mercer Street.

When Richard shows me the two Cubist Picassos hanging on the walls of his New York *flat*, he says:

- One of them is a fake. I was present when my father bought it from a forger. Guess which one is genuine!

I am wrong. I am offended to death. He's having fun with it:

- Well, even the greatest connoisseurs - experts - would be bluffed. Nevertheless, you must admit that it is disgusting to buy a fake Picasso for a derisory price and to resell it a hundred times its price after having obtained a positive expertise from the rightful owners!

I don't find it repulsive. To tell you the truth, I find it rather absurd. I know more and more about the art market. I know that no matter what happens to the economy, this market will always be more and more prosperous. Richard knows that I make Chagalls, Mirós, drawings by Toulouse-Lautrec, minor works by Matisse and Picasso, interpretations that easily pass expert examination and are thus rendered authentic. Now, if Richard has never been concerned about his livelihood, I am not. Hardly a materialist and seriously allergic to the politics of profit, I don't count: I just want to earn a lot and quickly, while having fun.

We hang up the finished fakes. They are a perfect illusion. In any case, they will never be put on sale. The real paintings - private collection, heritage accumulated thanks to the financial benefits and actions of the American-Fulton railroad - as well as the numerous certificates of authenticity, are insured and packed at Hudson Shipping.

Direction Tel-Aviv. Our collectors, contacted beforehand, are eager to buy these well-known and highly coveted works. They will thus fill their private museum with unobtainable pieces, halluci-

6. FULTON STREET: MATISSE, PICASSO AND CÉZANNE [1983]

nating in their rarity, not with the aim of profit but of accumulation intended for their descendants. *No risk of* finding them before decades on the international market. Too conservative and rich, our customers! The *masterpieces* arrived in excellent condition in Tel Aviv, at the David-Ben-Gurion airport cargo hold. A few days later, the El Al Airlines flight drops us off to finalize the secret transactions.

Once the pieces had been analyzed and the documents authenticated, we were paid for all the works by separate bank transfers: Richard's to UBS in Geneva, into a secret account; my share to Credit Suisse in Lausanne, an anonymous numbered account. The two Matisse, Tangiers odalisques, brought us the equivalent of 2.25 million dollars; the two cubist Picassos, 1.75 million dollars; the Renoir "only" 800,000 dollars; the Cézanne drawing, 600,000. In total, we split $5.46 million, 60% to Richard, 30% to me, and 10% cash to Helmut. When the deal was done, we suggested to our Tel Aviv collectors that they would have priority in purchasing other high quality works in the future.

The Fulton collection is known to collectors of the Jewish religion all over the world. It is therefore highly sought after from Israel to Boston (at least). Our collectors will continue to buy "our" works, keeping them for their personal enjoyment and for the quality of their investment. *Next time soon, friends!*

7. Mrs. Gould: Ernst, Giacometti and Miró [1984]

One day, Richard takes me to visit a friend of his family, Mrs. Gould. She lives alone in her large villa on the water, a stone's throw from the Palm Beach Casino in Cannes. She opens her heart to us and tells us the story of her life. Without any compensation (what compensation could we offer her?), she gives us access to her fabulous address book. Even without that, we love her. She was a diva of the Fitzgerald years of the Riviera. What does it matter if this diva is no longer sheltered from the time that sinks her; she drowns her days by squandering her fortune on the green carpets of Palm Beach, always *driven by* her faithful bodyguard, chauffeur and handyman. This guy, we call him Mr. Nocomment. Maybe he is mute, or even deaf? It doesn't matter!

Mrs. Gould had been the lover of Richard's wealthy grandfather. She waited until her last days to confess it to her descendant. We can only imagine the merger they must have experienced in their golden years! Today, Mrs. Gould wishes to reveal her soul, to let us know her relationships and especially to pass on to us a relay that the great ones of this world pass on from generation to generation, in a closed circle. *Very closed!* She encourages us to position ourselves as key players in the great international art market that her contacts govern. She exposes to us the arcana, the rules to respect and the art of playing with the best *players*. If, as she hopes, we aspire to become part of the circle of the greatest collectors, we will have to play ever more finely in ever tighter games.

Angel-goddess, almost hit and run, our mentor is the only captain of the thousand-square-meter villa-ship that starts to take water. Mr. Nocomment, the bodyguard that no one covets anymore, tries to plug the gaps. Until the end, he will remain the voiceless shadow, lost in an eternal absolute: that of the *openable*, the Gould, the divine, the extravagant who bequeathed to the State of Israel her collections of ancient and modern classical art and her fabulous 1930s furniture, matching the architecture of the villa built in the 1920s. Hop, gift! The rest of her financial assets will be divided between the city of Cannes, the city of Juan-les-Pins, the green carpets of Monte-Carlo and those of the Palm Beach, in Cannes.

What makes the business of art *dealing*, clone making, and fake-real art extraordinary is that it can be made illustrious through the most colorful natural anti-conformism. The adventure is in these different interpenetrated worlds, the occult markets, the *underground* finance, the laundering, the legal loopholes due to the cosmopolitanism of the laws of the art trade, the voluptuousness, the libertinage, the freedom and the mixture of genres. In my own scrambling of the cards, the mixture of the real, the fake and the false real has developed my humor, the one that ridicules the laws by my great airs and my sense of provocation, behind which are buried my shyness, my shamelessness and those vices that attract those who want to play with me by my rules. Crazy morals!

Closer to the *beat generation* than to *the* crazy *money makers*, I have to be first in the collimator of these *addicts collectors* while being able to solicit, for my defense, unknown but powerful plastic friends supporters of my work, of my means to exist and to express myself. My plastic art: the non-being understood as a methodically

maintained madness. The domain of Flossane begins to empty itself at the frantic rhythm of our ultra expensive trains of life, of our
pressing daily needs. This is measured by the length of the white
lines that we constantly cross, armor rails that protect us from the
negative waves of this gloomy reality.

Remake of the Park Avenue looting: Diva Gould having given
us access to most of her most important relations - bankers-col-
lectors -, all that remains is for us to get back to our work as forgers. Helmut comes to the rescue with his magic equipment and
his talent. Helmut, Richard and I choose and analyze the works to
be cloned. Destination: Tel Aviv! *First class! For* a while, Richard's
mother and his father-in-law, ex-minister of I don't know what
under Pompidou, take refuge in their castle in Touraine, one of
their luxurious caves, and leave us free to organize the cloning.

Once the inventory was complete, we chose only works from
this century. Miró and Chagall were friends of the Fultons and re-
gulars in the house, so we had plenty of them. Our new cloning
project focused on : two mixed oils by Alberto Giacometti, one
depicting a gaunt bust of a nude woman, the other a self-portrait
of the artist's emaciated face; also by Giacometti, six small-format
study drawings, quick to complete in graphite and India ink; two
medium-format gouaches by Marc Chagall done in Saint-Paul de
Vence, as well as five washes on paper and three oils by this master;
two oils on canvas by Miró, *The Port, 1945* and *Characters, Bird,
Star,* from 1946, major works by the Catalan painter; two other
works by the same Miró, more recent, *Woman and Bird in the Night*
from 1968, and *Silence* from 1968; as well as a small collage by Max
Ernst from 1921, titled *Loplop,* from the Dadaist-Surrealist period

It all starts with Richard's desire to pretend to plunder his own
legacy. His goal? To get back at his mother, who cheated him out
of a fortune estimated at hundreds of millions of dollars. Indeed,
when Richard's father died, with the help of crooked lawyers and

7. Mrs. Gould: Ernst, Giacometti and Miró [1984]

notaries just as rotten, Mom Fulton invented false wills leaving some crumbs to her son, enough to incite him to suicide. Richard felt humiliated, dependent on his stepmother and deprived, since his mother's remarriage, of his rightful share. With our help, he intends to get his revenge. Just return of the things!

Helmut and I begin the work of copying and cloning. It takes us several weeks to assemble the stretchers, to wear out the canvases, to dirty them with vacuum cleaner dust in order to age them, to adapt the colors to the different painters - no two painters used the same pigments, the same oils or the same tubes. Helmut takes great pleasure in executing the oils and gouaches perfectly, in detail. I take care of all the works on paper and the collage. I look for old magazines from that time, journals and newspapers in which I find the necessary material for the composition of "Max Ernst 1921". On the spot, the conditions are optimal: we have the sun, the time to have fun, white lines in industrial quantity and colored shadows.

From time to time, the servants come to organize receptions, buffets, alcohol and wine tastings. Once or twice a week, we have another bunch of crazy, hard-core party people with bimbos and friends. We get high: unbridled sex, a pool full of loaded nymphomaniacs, all for two or three days and nights, so as not to lose sight of our objective - pleasure. Crazy epicureans, we come down from our wild parties until our fragmented minds reposition themselves. From pure pleasure to *fun* cloning! Soon, the finished, aged, dried clones will take the place of the originals, which will still be leaving Nice, via Air France Cargo, for Israel.

Once he was back in the right place, Helmut tackled Giacometti's two oil paintings head on. After removing the frame, he installed ultra powerful spotlights to illuminate the originals and his own in the process of being made. The advantage of the heat of the spotlights is also that it makes the layers of oil paint dry more quickly. After treating the backgrounds, Helmut draws the two portraits: that of the emaciated female bust, as well as that of Alberto Giacometti, a face close to that of a figure emerging from a camp. Both works are made with the same materials. Only the subjects differ. It only takes Helmut three days to make them perfect, aged with ash, dust and heat.

On the Ruhlmann table, I am dealing with the six Giacometti studies. They are portraits of men and women, six small formats. I put the sheets, which are too white, in very strong, boiling tea; I dry them with a hair dryer and iron them. All that remains is to work on them. I am used to the speed of Giacometti's line and his signature. I master them perfectly. I do four of them with graphite, which has the advantage of dirtying the paper; the other two I treat with Indian ink and pen to the point of almost scratching and piercing the paper because of the repetition of the lines. I don't miss any of the six studies, although I have planned ten extra sheets, just in case.

A few bottles of coke later, I stop; Helmut too. It's time to take a *break*. After having framed all the Giacometti, oils and drawings under original glass, we go back to the "Tapir vacuum cleaner" effect, as usual. *Fiesta!* The omens are bright and lucrative. Alcoholic, Richard, Helmut and I track down, with an exacerbated eye, a too visible error which could have annihilated this titanic work.

Coming back down two days after us, Helmut tackles Chagall's gouaches, with aging of the paper in tea and drying. An afternoon later, the trick is done. The gouaches represent characters and circus animals, a subject dear to Chagall. He immediately moved on to the making of the three paintings of the master, one of which was from the Russian period, the most difficult to make, with a stretcher and a canvas of the period - we had to go to all the antique shops and flea markets to find some crusts from that period. Helmut manages very well. He also uses pigments mixed with a

7. Mrs. Gould: Ernst, Giacometti and Miró [1984]

special oil - I can't remember exactly which one, Helmut's secret! This time it takes a week to finish the canvas. The colors were aged under the flames of soldering lamps, again adding dust that set in the slightly fresh color. The work of the copyist was titanic, but the result is amazingly true. It takes the place of the real Russian lands-cape. The real ones, Richard carefully wraps them in bubble wrap. He ordered from a carpenter in Vence a protected box to contain all the original works and their certificate of authenticity.

In the wake of this, Helmut produced the other two works by Chagall, the Saint-Paul period, very colorful, sunny, views of the village, on the theme of lovers, bouquet of flowers in hand. The technique is simpler, because the materials that we find nowadays in the color shops are the same as those used by the master. As for aging, since the works were created at the end of the painter's life, around 1950-1960, I use them sparingly. Richard, now devotes himself to one and only one activity: laying out his tracks. As a conscientious station master, he rarely leaves his signal box.

For my part, I take care of the Chagalls on tea-yellowed paper: five washes, Indian ink and water, quick sketches with women ri-ders, circus characters, Saint Paul landscapes with lovers. A day la-ter, thanks to the drying speed of the ink, I can reframe them and re-hang them with the others on the picture rails of the large sa-lon in Flossane. I place the originals in strong drawing boxes, pro-tecting them with crystal paper dividers. I counted the number of paintings: all that remained was to produce the two oil paintings by Miró, *circa* 1940. Helmut sent them off in four days, including drying, while I tackled the Mirós on paper at top speed. Always the same principles of light tea aging, mixed techniques, gouache, pas-tels, charcoal, Indian ink traced directly with a finger dipped in ink. I have seen Miró work through films shown at the Maeght Founda-tion in Saint-Paul. He uses only his fingers dipped in ink or color, unless he scatters projections on his sheets with brushes until he achieves a perfect balance.

On the back, the gouaches and mixed media are embellished with inscriptions in ink or graphite. They mention the titles - *Mújeres en la noche, Silencio,* and *Mújeres pájaros en la noche* - and the date: 1968. I have no major difficulty in tracing Max Ernst's 1921 *Loplop* character, originally drawn with a ruler and compass, in graphite. All I have to do is glue the cut pieces of old paper on the character and on part of the background. The only problem is not to leave visible traces of glue when I have plenty of it on my fingers! Anyway, a few hours later, *Loplop was* back in its original glass frame, in the right place; and the original joined all the works on paper in the protective box.

With our work done, we get down to business: organizing party after party around and in the pool, outside and inside the estate. A hundred of Jaimie's friends, *girls* and *gays,* come to stay for a week to have sex on the different planets of their choice. The caterers, in constant activity, finally relax and join us, in the mess of offbeat bodies and minds that tape a Flossane upside down. Shortly after, all the works join the *safebox* that Richard will nevertheless control at the freight. Our forgeries leave insured, protected and accompanied by certified copies of the documents. Everything is square. As for the large living room, it has been - only partially - reclassified and *redesigned in* an undetectable way. At least we hope so...

8. The price of a work: Bellmer, Soutine and Modigliani [1985]

Richard, Helmut and I are still congratulating ourselves on the results of our hard work when Fulton Mam comes into the large living room. She is surprised to see that her "heir of a son", Helmut and I, are speculating about the quality of the collection assembled by the railroaders. We are equally astonished to see her. Did it arrive on a flying fish? Her appearance stuns us... and clearly makes us uncomfortable. Fulton is no more assured. She thinks our only interests in life are to perch high. She sees us as constant weirdos, constantly smearing our drugs on the table closest to us. To her, our bawdy friends are our only way of existing. She's wrong, but not that wrong.

Just to pull myself together, I grabbed a few Lexomil from the bottom of my pockets and swallowed them in one go with a glass of Absolut. Richard, pretending to have an emergency, climbs the Roger Tallon stairs leading to his cartel to charge himself with energy. *Coke - no diet!* As for Helmut, he finished his bottle of Russian vodka of clandestine manufacture. Alas, the glass of the bottle is still impregnated with all the colors of his palette, betraying the sleight of hand he just performed.

A chalice of Chablis in hand, not fooled by our behavior, the Fulton decides to put our artistic knowledge to the test. Among the paintings in the collection, signed by David Teniers the Younger, Delacroix, Arcimboldo, Braque cubist, Picasso, Chagall, Miró, Dufy, Mondrian, Bellmer and so many other masters of the 17th and 18th centuries, would we know which works were authentic and which were not? Panic! Richard, Helmut and I go into vibrate mode. I don't want her doubts to be confirmed and allow her to accuse us of heritage theft. Did she realize she was being deceived? She questions me, staring at me while emptying her glass of Chablis. For long minutes, I look for support from Helmut and Richard. Luckily, the Fulton comes up dry. While she pours herself half a bottle of her favorite vintage white, I run to sniff fifty centimeters of *contessa blanca* to boost myself.

So I play poker with it, eye to eye. The Fulton is pretty much gone after three glasses of Chablis, emptied in less time than it takes to write this. The matron keeps her balance, but standing seems to be almost painful for her. The *contessa* which circulates in me gives me the appearance of imperturbable firmness, that of the truth-lie.

I point out all the modern works we have cloned and replaced as being of high quality, claiming however not to be an expert in modern art. Then I point out the Picassos, Braques and Dufys that we have not reworked as being, "despite my limited knowledge", 100% authentic. Finally, I express great reservations about the old works, explaining that I have neither taste nor great knowledge of these periods which, according to me, are of no interest.

To celebrate my diagnosis, Richard runs to his private cartel to restore his neurons, leaving the Chablis chalice to confer with Helmut's clandestine, multicolored bottle of Russian vodka. I wait for the verdict while sipping my glass of Absolut. Did the intruder bite on the big *bluff* I served her? Will the queen mother be angry, drunk from having drunk two bottles alone? After an interminable apnoea, drowning a fish out of water, the Fulton collapses on the 1930's sofa and starts to tell me (what I already knew) by stammering that her husband - Richard's father - and his forefathers accumulated this collection thanks to the Stock Exchange.

- Richard's father bought all his works from the artists themselves, in their studios," she says, pointing to my clones. Miró and Chagall often had dinner in Flossane...

She points out the Giacomettis, also cloned, and all the other works we had not taken an interest in, all of which were considered true by the Fulton. Conclusion: she saw nothing but fire in our shenanigans. The pressure is slowly coming down.

As for the old works, she admits to me:

- You know, Eric, Richard's great grandfather acquired almost all of these masters from the seventeenth to the twentieth century, buying both real and fake works, executed during the artist's lifetime, with the blessing of the master who allowed his friends to profit from his fame and signature. This has often happened in the history of art... Moreover, the certificates authenticating the pieces, it is always the master who signed them to recognize as being of him a work that he had not executed! All these works were bought for a few hundred dollars a hundred to a hundred and fifty years ago. The Soutines? Acquired from the painter himself for wine and food for a few weeks... or less! These two Modigliani? Bought at the same time in Paris, on canvas, of excellent quality, reproduced today in the catalog raisonné made by Patani and also sold by Modi for almost nothing. The Soutine-Modigliani duo, frustrated and suicidal, I'm-a-freak, accepted everything, 1920s oblige!

Richard goes back down for the umpteenth time. He stumbles, misses a step on the Tallon staircase and almost falls down.

- Don't be surprised, Richard, Eric didn't make a mistake! Anyone could have been fooled, though. Even the experts I appointed for the division of this pictorial heritage and for the to-

8. THE PRICE OF A WORK: BELLMER, SOUTINE AND MODIGLIANI [1985]

tal evaluation of our movable and immovable goods, they were fooled...

Truth ? Is it a lie? We will never know!

- Admit it, Richard, that it is not wrong to buy a period fake, even one recognized as authentic by the masters themselves, for that little bit of food money, when they did not know the work that bore their signature! So, you, one day, can resell these paintings for several tens of millions of dollars...

Neither Richard, who had asked me about the fake Picassos in the New York *flat*, nor his mother, when talking about the fake real works that were prominently displayed in the Saint Paul estate, had any real problems of conscience. They were only interested in the money, the rest was a thing of the past; in any case, all the works were certified true by the experts of each of the masters.

The heir, Helmut and I remain slumped on the Toshiyuki Kita jute sofas, largely dusted by the old coke accumulated in the fibers of their Nippon fabric. I call my inner strength rebooted by the *contessa blanca* to stay on my pleasure planet. I want to enjoy the success of our *bluffs* while dreaming of the days of celebration in Tel Aviv which are coming! Alas, I have a doubt. After all, haven't we made clones of fake works, even authenticated ones? Well, what does it matter? It's too late to question this amount of hard work. The certificates will preserve us from bad surprises.

Nevertheless, we had to pull some rails to manage what could have become an international scandal, a resounding fiasco and the beginning of a dark nightmare! In Tel Aviv, our collectors are not kidding. To counterbalance this anxiety, we assume our nature as tapirs, and use our minitrompe to breathe in the white lines that brighten up the marble of the 18th century chest of drawers stamped Biennais - the cabinetmaker of Louis XVI and Marie-Antoinette. The marquetry of the Ruhlmann table was *destroyed* because of the lacerations of our blades, which were used to trace our ephemeral writings, those of our vices. Good to restore!

New graphics, new lives! The Richard, completely on the edge of breaking, mumbles:

- Eric, what makes a work of art expensive?

I decree:

- Twenty percent the name of the artist, thirty percent the quality of the work, fifty percent the reputation of the owner of the collection.

- More and more absurd, mutters the heir.

9. My Dufy period [1985]

I have become an art pirate. To pay for my numerous addictions, I take a tortuous path, at the risk of creating problems of conscience and small conflicts with the repression of frauds, the taxman and the specialists of the counterfeiting in artistic matter. The drug makes me forget these problems. Ah, white peace, when you hold us!

I start working on my own works. I made a stock of scenes of the Riviera in the 1930s, based on the original works of Raoul Dufy that I had spotted at the Fulton villa in Saint-Paul. Like my first forgery, these drawings and gouaches express the moods of racetracks, studies of public gardens like Albert I's in Nice, with women in crinolines, children playing, carousels of horse-drawn carriages walking the light idleness of wealthy exiles in the sunny South of France. I noticed an authentic oil painting hanging in the villa, purchased directly from Dufy by Richard's father. It was called *Reception at the Élysée*. I know that it is valued at six to seven hundred thousand euros. I suggest to Richard to go and see the experts. They live in the Villa Dufy, right on the water in the splendid harbor of Villefranche-sur-Mer. Richard listens to me, drawing large lines of coke on the Louis XIV Boulle marquetry. He is overexcited at the idea that the authentic oil mixed with my false studies will be presented to the rightful owners.

We went to the Dufy villa. We came across two servants and a friend of the painter who, squatting in the villa, had set herself up as an expert. On all the walls of the five hundred square meters of space are hung hundreds of works unknown to the public, all part of the heritage of the estate of Raoul Dufy.

Once this ultra rewarding private visit is accomplished, we present Richard's famous oil painting, indisputable, and my five studies, each one as fake as the next. During the analysis of these works, we start to feel the descent, black runway version. The expert taking ages to appraise, we take it in turns to boost ourselves discreetly.

The expert's smile betrays her interest in all of our drawings and paintings, especially *Reception at the Élysée*. She explains to us the circumstances under which each work was created, as well as the reasons why Dufy placed a particular color there rather than elsewhere, and how he conceived the balance of the compositions. She is charmed. Intoxicated by dreams of speculative and personal enrichment, she offers to buy everything for the paltry sum of 300 000 €. We decline the proposal, asking her simply for the certificates authenticating the six pieces. She wrote them on the back of the photos I had previously taken. Thanking her for this constructive afternoon, we promise to give her some of our works for sale as a priority.

The *Reception at the Elysium* resumes its place in Flossane. I sell to an enlightened amateur the five forgeries that have become, by our magic, definitively true. The equivalent of 400 000 € appear at once on my usual account in Switzerland. A few years later, I will see the Dufy studies at public auction in Hamburg at three times the price I sold them for. This is a good thing! On my side, I skimmed the public sales and acquired for my personal collection a Monet representing the cliff of Étretat, red, yellow, blue, green - a late summer afternoon, certainly. Richard receives his share in an account in Tel Aviv. He reinvests in astronomical quantities of coke and heroin. I can't keep up. What is he looking for? What world does he want to go to? To Wonderland, without the rabbit? Drunk, I spin around like a dervish, in an accelerated sense of excess.

It was then that I had the opportunity to recover a hundred Chagalls, *through* a friend who knew very well the janitor of the villa "La Colline" of the late Chagall, in which we would organize memorable evenings a few years later. This poor house was haunted by the ghosts of the works taken down by the State, to pay the inheritance tax and other taxes. One day, the son of the janitor turned off the alarm and opened the sacrosanct studio of the master. There was not a single canvas left in the vertical racks that were used to store them. Barely thirty or so gouaches and drawings scattered all over the place, on the floor, pinned to the wall, accumulated in the corners of the studio. These preparatory works, not always finished, did not attract the covetousness of the Ministry of Culture. I spotted two large format books, bound, lying on the work table and forgotten, as well as a hundred or so signed and numbered lithographs, dusty like everything else that was there.

I ask my friend why this mess. He answers that he doesn't care because he doesn't know anything about it! His only concern:

- Do you have any idea what these two books are worth?

I leaf through them and see that they are illustrated with lithographs and poems. These are two very rare copies of *Daphnis and Chloé* intended for the artist and signed Marc Chagall. There were only thirty copies, which must be in large private collections. The answer is therefore: a million dollars, at least, on the international market. In addition, there are still a hundred numbered and signed lithographs, still on the theme of Daphnis and Chloe, which were not used to produce the works.

I pick up the phone and call Christie's, Lithographs and Prints Department. They confirm that, if the books are in perfect condition, the price of one million dollars is a floor, as these works have not been on the market for several years. Better still, they offered to show them to me, as they thought they could make me a much higher offer. A dream come true! Except that I don't want to be the last bird of prey behind the state. I ask if the heirs are willing to sell them... and I learn that they don't know about them!

I leave the two books on the spot. I propose to my contact to buy back all the drawings and gouaches that are deteriorating, as well as the hundred or so lithographs left over. I offer him the equivalent of 30 000 € in cash. This is what I have at home without having to go to Switzerland or Luxembourg. Inveterate cocaine addict, he accepts against the promise to pay him another thirty thousand euros if I sell them correctly. We agree. He takes his share, and I find myself again in a state of advanced overexcitement. I have to analyze about one hundred and forty works, clean them up, put them back on the shelf and restore those papers that must have been trampled. The light illuminates me with the yellow and the famous blue that Chagall used in his years in Saint Paul.

I take the opportunity to make copies and then try to sell real and fake Chagalls plus a few other works in the process. My companion of the moment helps me to sell some to an antique dealer in Nice who works regularly with the Fulton family. I knew the father very well, Mr. Cerroni, who had unfortunately passed away. My friend introduced herself to her son Michel as the heir and asked him if he was interested in these works. When asked about the provenance of the works, she did not know what to say. She was asked for the title deeds, the notarial succession, the deeds. Too stressed, she gave up, found me at the Meridian, returned the works and told me that she had left my name as the person who had indicated to her this dealer on the rue de France, without, of course, saying that they were forgeries by my hand.

Panic takes me, and rightly so. The next day, at the golden villa, on the heights of Cannes, I have the right to a search. The police found about thirty works in bulk, paintings that I was used to doing, plus works of my own. I am taken away. The cops are convinced that they are stolen paintings. Here I am handcuffed in the premises of the Nice police. After two hours of interrogation about the provenance, furious that I didn't recognize anything except that these pieces belonged to me, the cops pulled out all the stops: either I drooled, or they arrested my friend, a fragile heroin addict. I play their game, just to avoid this ordeal to this girl's love. To the great displeasure of the policemen, I explain to them that it is me who painted everything. Of course, nobody takes me seriously. Not credible, Eric! So, from memory, with a Bic pen and a few sheets of machine paper, I redid a Dufy - the drawing of the garden with the carriage -, a Miró and a sketch of Chagall that they had taken from my house.

Astonishment! Almost by chance, the police got their hands on, as the regional press *Nice-Catin* would say, "the father of the false Chagalls". My photo, that of a Miró and that of a Chagall, appear on the front page, followed by a delirious article. The press gets carried away and headlines: "Arrest of the king of the brush, emperor of the forgery".

The class, so to speak.

10. My Matisse period [1985]

I only read these articles after my arrival at the Nice prison. The guards and inmates welcome me with a smile. I am rather woozy: the cops offered me a lot of champagne to celebrate my arrest. I am still in the blur of bubbles. To incriminate me, the examining magistrate is obliged to review his law courses. Going back to the Napoleonic code, he extracted a 19th century law on artistic forgery, forgery and intellectual property rights. I risk two years in prison and the equivalent of a €300,000 fine.

So I chose the best lawyer, a collector and friend of César, Gérard Baudoux. He uses all possible weapons to defend me - I am an artist after all! In court, he brilliantly admitted that the real forgers, and this since the dawn of time, are the experts and the dealers, who are supposedly unable to be mistaken about the origin of the works and their authenticity. Moreover, their profits are much higher than those of the artist-forger, namely four to ten times more at the resale. However, he points out, "this law of the market does not apply to a private individual who buys a Rodin 100 000 € to resell it 10 or 15 times more expensive. Professionals are bound to an 'honest' profit margin, not individuals, for whom this legal loophole can be a winning lottery ticket." Luckily for me, no real work, no certificate, no money was found. No civil party has come forward despite the calls for witnesses in the local newspaper. I've paid for ten months, I saved my girlfriend, I assume the rest.

The prison of Nice is squalid, unhealthy and unlivable. All kinds of trafficking reign there. I organize myself as best I can in the middle of this fauna of robbers, pimps and guards: the prison system, in short! In this closed world where black emotions shine, there is no place for empty relationships. I take care of mine to avoid sinking, to overcome my losses, my frustrations and my disappointments, and to maintain the hope of finding, one day, the light.

During these ten months of detention, I start to paint works on the prison universe but also great Miró, Picasso and Lautrec, for some kings and guards. The inmates decorate their cells like an art gallery. A friend of misfortune, Francis the Belgian, fills his cell with various Chagalls, his favorite painter - he has real ones, by the way, he tells me. Some of the wardens order me Toulouse-Lautrec; in return, I get alcohol, cigars and all sorts of indispensable food. As a bonus, I gained the freedom to move around during the day. The hacks provide me with brushes, colors and canvases. They bring me art books from which they choose their subjects. The director herself orders paintings for her apartment. In short, I try to have fun, in spite of this sordid place that I try to decorate as best I can.

Above all, I am almost at peace. I kill time by painting and, by doing so, I obtain some privileges reserved for the "elite", in other words for the kingpins of the big banditry. Free in spite of my confinement, I go from one building to another to play chess, cards, backgammon with the top guys. Moreover, it is thanks to chess - I play it almost every day - that I meet Anthony Tannoury, a French-Lebanese businessman. The man is a big collector of impressionism and modern art. Before being imprisoned for tax evasion, he lived between Lebanon, the French Riviera, Paris and New York. He owned dozens of *offshore* companies and had no shortage of connections in the international *jet set.* The press had nicknamed him "the sulphurous billionaire". For me, he was a partner in wild games, in which we bet big. During a game, he proposed a crazy deal that he thought was feasible. The plan is as follows: when I leave, he lends me his Central Park apartment so that I can make Matisse paintings from the Azure period, Picassos from the Blue period and Modiglianis. He provided me with the originals; it was up to me to find the canvases, the stretchers, the colors, everything that was needed to make them "period" and, above all, the literature of the catalogs raisonnés of each of these masters. Once the works were made, he took charge of transporting them to one of his properties in Cyprus. There, he had them insured by a Saudi company for twenty million dollars. Afterwards, he has his villa blown up by Lebanese terrorists: he considers this end credible because, on the one hand, he is a Christian and, on the other hand, his father was a high official in Lebanon after the outbreak of the Iran-Iraq war. The objective is of course to get the biggest part of the insurance that we would share, 40% for him, 40% for me, 20% for the swindling Saudi insurer and the villa dynamiters, accomplices of this dangerous and very lucrative enterprise. The exoticism of the project seduces me. I accept, demand and obtain an advance of $200,000.

When I got out of prison, things got a little more complicated. In New York, I have to move into a hotel because Anthony's apartment, his *jet*, his *boats* and a lot of other things have been seized by the IRS. Despite this, I am excited to return to the fast-paced, hectic, crazy life I love so much in this megalopolis; and I start working on the project we agreed on. I waste an impressive number of canvases before succeeding in two Matisse paintings from the Venice period. Aware of my limitations, I call Helmut to the rescue. No luck: he is drowned in his homemade vodkas. So I have to try my hand at the other works commissioned by "Tony the Magnificent", as he is now called by the

10. My Matisse period [1985]

celebrity magazines. This work is not new to me, but I lack the desire and the energy. I spend hours, days, nights hanging out in bars and clubs, getting drunk on sounds, alcohol, sex and drugs. I wake up with bimbos I don't know, even though I've partied with them for two or three nights, scouring the trendy and hot spots of this city that never stops. To make matters worse, I am alerted by a close friend, who also knows Tannoury: according to him, once my contract is fulfilled, I might never get paid. Some friends have experienced the dark side of the tycoon. Moreover, the man really smells of sulfur. It is said that he sold weapons to Iraq, helicopter gunships to Iran and nuclear missiles to Libya. Without being a coward, I think that being involved in this kind of traffic deserves reflection. So, calmly, I take stock.

This project interested me above all for the challenge it represented. After a period of inactivity, it allowed me to put my abilities to the test. Was I still capable of completing a mission perfectly? In part, yes. But I have no intention of risking my life for it. So I decided to stick with the two Matisse. I received the agreed advance, Tony and I are even. I have my forgeries shipped from New York by Hudson Shipping, my usual forwarder. In Cyprus, as agreed, his brother and secretary receive the works. I specify that our collaboration ends there. Tannoury is furious. I explain to him that I am a painter, just a painter and, in spite of the interest of this enriching work, I do not want to get involved with arms trafficking.

Then I leave New York.

11. My Miró period [1986]

Back in Saint Paul, I started to work more seriously on my own works, forgetting the absurd world in which I was evolving. Eighteen months for a few forgeries is still a lot of money! I contact Leo Castelli, Mary Boone and other renowned galleries... and I meet their incomprehension: they are only interested in conceptual art. Despite this failure, I persist. I dream of selling or, *at least, of* presenting my ideas and concepts to the general public. I work on my painting and paint on huge boat sails, very colorful pieces, which I exhibit mainly on the French Riviera, in Saint-Paul, Vence and Tourrettes-sur-Loup, as well as in Denmark and Norway, where there are many marinas. Owners of *sailing boats* buy my work to hang on the walls of their villas or apartments. The result is imposing, rich in colors and materials, in short: perfect for Northern Europe. Of course, I don't sell them for enough money to make a living; nevertheless, I have the pleasure of making those who collect them happy. Nevertheless, when they ask for more, the prices being too low, I prefer to offer them. A boat sail, even a worn one, costs a small fortune, more than what I sell it for painted. Without ruling out the possibility of resuming my production of fakes, I prefer to develop my own work.

On large canvases, at least 160x190 cm, I create about fifty acrylic paintings to prepare an exhibition in Paris. Denise, the companion of my lawyer at the time, introduces me to a young Italian art lover who opens his first gallery near the Avenue Georges V. He liked my work very much. We signed at Baudoux. Our agreement was encouraging: the exclusivity contract committed me to producing a quantity of one hundred large-format pieces per year, with an advance on revenues so as to live and pay for raw materials, frames, canvases, the studio... And, indeed, as agreed, the gallery owner paid me the equivalent of 30,000 € in advance and offered me full-page advertisements in the magazine *L'œil*. Except that it is a smoke screen. A few months later, he loaded a truck with almost all of my work and exhibited it in his gallery without paying me a cent. Shortly after, I learned that he had organized his fraudulent bankruptcy. I never saw my titanic work again, these guts thrown on disappeared canvases. Today, I only have about thirty of them left. To appease my disgust, I tell myself that the second cover of *L'œil*, on three consecutive issues, reproduced the image of my paintings on glossy paper. Little comfort.

The hypocritical merchant-businesses disgust me. In France, they share their gigabenefits with two categories of people: the experts and the holders of the so-called moral right, for dead artists. This "immoral" right is used to cover up tax fraud, the evasion of fortunes and the laundering of money of mafia origin. In New York, Seoul or Shanghai, the essence of their success is based on unconcealed greed. Art is the lubricant of the *intelligentsia* and the financial world.

Obliged, I fall back into the false-money-loss spiral with a power and a supercharged niaque. I attack César, Nolde, Kirchner, Miró and all those who, like Fernand Léger, are sold in two minutes after two hours of work. Hatred increases my energy tenfold and the desire to not depend on anyone, especially not on galleries and auctioneers. I become a *serial* forger. No pride: I don't like series and their laws. The realization of my forgeries - drawings, paintings, gouaches, sculptures - costs me nothing, except energy, desire, paper, metal, canvas and concentration.

Long after the success of the Mirós in the Fulton collection, I immerse myself in the work of this master in order to dissect it and understand the life of the painter. I decided to spend my time in libraries, museums and cinematheques to collect everything that spoke to me about Miró or showed him working. I take notes and photos. I film the screenings, the film copies, the reports that are not on the market. From the Maeght Foundation to the Miró Foundation in Barcelona, from the outskirts of his property "Son abriñes, Calamajor" in Palma de Mallorca to the Solomon R. Guggenheim Museum in New York and from the Chicago Art Institute to the Kunstmuseum Basel in Basel, I hunt for a mass of information. My goal: to interpret new works that bring together the same discourses and signs as Miró's, and to complete my personal research on the Catalan master's Majorcan introspection in three months.

In Düsseldorf, a collector opens his house to me, where works such as *Nude with Mirror* from 1919 and the oil on canvas titled *The Table, Still Life with Rabbit* from 1920, teach me a lot. I am studying the geometric structures of these works, which are too old to be reworked but are important for understanding the evolution of Miró's work from the beginning to the end of his life. These structures, derived from Cubism, are combined with the painter's hyperrealist perception. Thus, the woman in the first painting expresses a mysterious calm and inner contemplation.

In my short life, I have seen many painters' and sculptors' studios - nothing like Miró working in his den. This place of creation offered a most curious spectacle: large and small easels, ladders, tables, stools, all in disorder, cluttered the studio. Large cut-out papers were spread out on the floor; stones and pottery held them in place. They were covered with those "signs" that Miró made so familiar. On the

11. My Miró period [1986]

black-and-white screen, I watched him enjoy laying out these paper symbols on the floor and moving them around, constantly creating new arrangements until the constellation from which his next painting would emerge. With his fingers dipped in black ink, he traced the essential lines representing the outline of his abstract subjects such as *Mújeres españolas, Mújeres y pájaros en la noche.* Inside the outline spaces, he used the bright and joyful colors of the child painter, those of Spain, those of the light of Palma, the sunny yellows, the bright reds, the light greens, the deep ultramarine blues.

I take the opportunity to spot the marks of his color tubes. I analyze his compositions, the evolution of these, not losing a detail of the ingredients, of his technique. I think of the moment when, in my turn, I will create with the same pleasure, new works on paper and on burlap. I will put them on sale in order to afford real ones for the pleasure of expanding my personal museum. I don't plan to do anything else than to penetrate Miró's mind. I want to assimilate the recipe of his creative *salsa*: powerful, light, childish, simple work. Not a canvas visible on the easel, not a sketch on the tables... Only the "signs" strewn on the floor testify to the long and slow elaboration of the work in progress. The "signs" on some papers look like they have been drawn for years! I accumulate all this precious information and immerse myself in his way of observing. The camera insists on his concentration and his way of examining, which constitute his attitude while he paints.

Then I take action. I find sheets and order from Palma the same brand of colors as Miró's. Then I made the first oil paintings on paper, lying on the floor of my mother's villa in Saint-Paul. I enter the page thoroughly to bring out, in two or three days, a first series of about fifty interpretations "in the spirit of Miró". I have fun just like him, but I go faster in execution because I am not encumbered by the doubt of the creator. I only miss the light of Palma, of Cataluña, of its yellows, reds and blacks; in spite of this, I give life to new *Pája-*

ros en la noche, Mújeres españolas, Mújeres catalanas en la noche, and *Pájaros en la noche mallorquine.*

I sign my works from the 1940s to the 1960s, titling them on the back, just as Miró did. I took pictures of the back of his frames to capture his writing, his strength and his speed. I studied the back of the Mirós, deciphered the provenance, the type of stretcher for the oils, and even the various labels tracing the route of the traveling exhibitions from museum to exhibition. Indeed, to authenticate it, the experts do not only rely on the quality of the work, on its aura, but also on the traceability that there is between the artist who made it and those who hold it.

Pretending to be a friend of the Fulton family, whose son was squandering the family collection, I made a first test sale in Monaco. I offered six pieces to Sotheby's and a few to various Italian galleries. All of them were bought for the equivalent of 50 000 to 100 000 € each. From then on, the gallery owners asked me if I had any others to sell. Out of my stock, I keep a few for memory, then I disperse about fifty in various galleries in Paris, Madrid, Nice and Saint-Paul with the Pascal Retelet gallery, which will be of great importance to me - euphemism - in the years to come.

In all, I create four hundred and fifty works by Miró. I disperse them in Boston and Tel Aviv, primarily among the friends of the Angel Gould, and in private collections in Norway and Denmark, where the light of the South is a necessity. Above all, I practice the exchange, the real forgeries against real works that I accumulate for my pleasure of aesthetic collector: Dufy, Chagall, Picasso, Léger, César and other Basquiat. I alternate the orders of forgeries that I realize at high speed, with the sale of authentic works in order to cover my tracks and to remain undetectable...

12. My Baldwin period [1987]

I was, as always, looking for major works when I had the good fortune to meet James Baldwin, the African-American writer and pastor, homosexual, author of the cult book *Less Than a Dog*. He lived in his villa in St. Paul with his friend Bernard, a former dancer with the Contemporary Dance Ballet in New York. James was an avid collector of *pop art* and New Realism from Nice. With him, I visited his collection and spotted the compressed sculptures made by César.

He told me about his political and religious stance, coming to the aid of African-Americans to be recognized as full citizens. Certainly all of Harlem agreed with him on this. His militancy and literary activism struck a chord in a racist world. When we met, he shared his ideas with me. He wanted to understand what I was thinking. We would debate American international politics and come to the conclusion that we have to fight all our lives to have our ideas and values taken into account. If Harlem dances one day, it will be because of him and his predecessors like Malcolm X and Martin Luther King.

James had an incurable cancer. I visited him constantly. I was convinced that he liked me. He listened to me, I listened to him. A short time later, he was dying. I supported him as best I could -

with my presence, my words, my life. I would have given him more if it had been possible. I brought him his newspapers, French and American, and freshly cut roses. They came from his beautiful rose garden, which I tried to maintain, as he could no longer do so. I picked the flowers, put them in vases, in short, I did my best, and it was not enough.

At his insistence, to fight his pain, I found him opiates, palfium, a little heroin. I was reluctant, not knowing what risk he was taking by consuming them. So I supplied him only sparingly. I wanted him to be at peace, without suffering! This went on for a long time, and then James died before my eyes and Bernard's.

Not wanting to leave anything to his eternally absent brother, and knowing that I liked his collection, James offered me some of his works. I refused, but I agreed to buy what he wanted to give me during his lifetime. So I paid him *cash for* two works by Yves Klein, a blue monochrome, a *post-mortem Victory of Samothrace*, printed in a few rare copies, and a pink sponge mounted on a stem with a stone base. I kept them in order to build up my collection and to tackle this master later on, even though I was aware that all these works had a great market value and were coveted by collectors and gallery owners *all over the world*.

On the other hand, James insisted on giving me drawings of César, portraits of him executed by César and dedicated "to my American darling", a book of photos in which we see him posing alongside César and other artists, photos taken in front of the Honda dealer in Nice who supplied César with new large motorcycles, Honda 750s that ended up with zero kilometers on the odometer, compressed, transformed into an abstract prism. Through James, I also obtained an insect, a scorpion in welded iron from the 1960's, now estimated to be worth at least 250,000 €, a rare sculpted-welded work from the time when César was learning sculpture. James also gave me five compressions that Caesar had given him: two beautiful 750 Honda compressions, a polychrome compression of empty paint tubes, a small red Ferrari-style pedal car with the number six, and a compression of Coke cans. In fact, I later learned that James had given me almost his entire private collection. His brother, having rejected James because of his political commitment to the black cause, would "only" have the property in St. Paul - what a property! Right in the middle of St. Paul, close to the galleries and the famous Golden Dove!

I was therefore the recipient of everything that could be unhooked. Indeed, James also gave me two drawings by Picasso, lead pencil on paper, *Nu de femme* and *Faunes dansant une ronde*; a work by Arman from 1968, *Le temps éclaté*, shattered pocket watches enclosed in an Epoxy resin prism. Arman spent his nerves on lots of objects that always ended up in resin and that he called "Colères d'Arman": violent aesthetics!

Other Arman works still represented anger, but on violins, exploded, shattered, burned with a blowtorch, pieces aesthetically recomposed and always included in resin prisms. The most beautiful work that James gave me for free was a work by Martial Raysse representing France, his wife at the time. It is a portrait in ultra flashy colors with the contours of the face and lips in neon, small tubes installed in the canvas, illuminating this painted face *pop art* style.

All of James' works represented a fortune, the equivalent of more than one million euros at the time. Today, probably ten times more. James, without formalizing it, had bequeathed it all to me with one goal: that no one else would get it. He knew that I lived partly for art. So I will always keep this parting gift in memory of a powerful friendship. I would make many Yves Kleins so as not to sell the real ones, and I would clone other works for the same reason. When I later got into serious trouble with the law, I had to reluctantly part with much of this fabulous collection. In the mean-

12. My Baldwin period [1987]

time, some of the works have gone to the safety of a free port in Geneva; others have adorned my walls, hanging on the walls of my successive flats.

The television channel Arte filmed and commented on James' funeral. They did a "special" for almost three hours on him, his action and his work for the black community. As my friend's body was brought home, the film showed that all of Harlem was there, in the church. A hundred times as many people had gathered outside. James' soul, his activism, and his writings will live on in the history of the struggle against African-American discrimination and in the defense of minority rights, along with the struggles of Angela Davis and the Black Panthers.

13. My first meetings with César [1989]

James Baldwin is the man who made me understand Caesar. He enlightened me on what lay behind his creation. The anecdotes he told me allowed me to penetrate the artist's mind and, later, to give credibility to my forgeries.

In the magazines about the School of Nice, one could find articles about César's first works, when he lived in the Belle de Mai, in Marseille, and was already known to love women. A man of strength and taste, he learned to weld his first sculptures in a garage near Marseilles, around 1955, from Mr. Roletto who helped him operate the electric arc, the forge and the various metalworking machines. These unique pieces are listed in Denyse Durand-Ruel's catalog of the master's work, but this catalog stops in 1964 and has not been updated.

At the end of the 1950s, César was not so well known that he became a driving instructor for ladies. On a yellow Dauphine, he taught his clients how to drive (and more if they liked, I guess). No wonder the first compressed cars were Dauphines! But he went far beyond that: he made many sculptures in welded iron, representing chickens, insects, scorpions, wasps, of all sizes... and self-portraits. These works are rare, almost impossible to find. Their prices reach the top, they are the most sought after.

To organize his first exhibitions, César placed his welded iron sculptures on pedestals. These pedestals were nothing less than large compressions recovered from car wrecks. History tells us that, at the opening, the collectors were just as fascinated by the compressed pedestals as by the iron sculptures. Moreover, the bases, prisms and cubes were not really cleaned. Oils and grease were dripping on the gallery floor. Compression was imposed in the minds. The New Realism then took off in Nice with Arman, Nicky de Saint Phalle, Robert Malaval, Ben and Pierre Restany, the group's theorist. In Nice and New York, two major creative movements were born. Paris was in the west! *Pop art* and New Realism were based on the same principle: to represent the society of that time, any consumer object, including stars, could do the trick by becoming iconic.

For my part, I started making compressions in a car wreck near Grasse, where I had gone with a friend, a professor of urban planning and close to the New Realists. I took photos of this end-of-the-world place. I had the impression of being crushed by floors of cars ready to be recycled, and not necessarily as works of art! I later learned that Caesar also frequented this junkyard.

The first car I pressed was decorated with a beautiful graphic. I bought it for 76.20 francs, at metal weight. I spent several days removing the visible traces of oil, grease and dust. It was a matter of giving it a decent aesthetic appearance. I then compressed it, signed it César and offered it to the Ferrero gallery in Nice. This dealer exchanged works of his artists for mine, not always true. As soon as he saw my work, the gallery owner got carried away by my amateurism. He explained to me in his usual manner that this compression *could* not be by Caesar, simply because it was just compressed aluminum, nothing more. Nothing to do with authentic compressions! When the artist compressed small cars, silver spoons or forks or even enamel coffee pots, all these objects, even compressed, were still recognizable.

I took note of it, and I offered my first try to an antique dealer in Nice. It was a relief, and I didn't imagine that I would have this failure appraised - I was proven wrong!

I met César the same year. I was invited to his home-workshop, a bric-a-brac in Roquefort-les-Pins, to take pictures of his sculptures. I watched and photographed him welding, picking up bits of scrap metal that ended up in magnificent sculptures. With a little, this genius created a realistic dream, palpable and *very expensive*!

Once my scouting was done, I started to make study drawings of centaurs, chickens with or without wheels, and self-portraits of the artist. As usual, I used the same materials, the most basic ones, Bic pens, Indian ink treated with a fountain pen, pencil with graphite, gouache, nail polish... Anything that fell under the hand of the master could be used to draw.

I reached my cruising speed: I was producing twenty to twenty-five a day. During his lifetime, César was reluctant to sell these drawings, except when he could ask a very high price for them. In a few months, I accumulated more than a thousand of them. I sold some of them on the markets and in galleries in Nice and Paris. As long as we did not exceed the equivalent of 3000 € per drawing, the antique dealers - antique dealers - dealers of Nice but also the European galleries, all wanted them. It didn't matter to them where they came from, how many there were or how authentic they were. My work was good, and there was nothing easier to do.

When word got out that works of art were being bought without an invoice and under the table, I did not panic. I began to prospect the galleries dealing with this period of art history in Saint-Paul. Pascal Retelet had the biggest gallery. He was greatly interested in acquiring, at unbeatable prices, new works by César, Miró, Alechinsky and Appel, even offering me advances to buy the works. I suggested to him that, since I was always in urgent need of money, I could be the bearer of works that were usually untouchable and, consequently, could be sold at exorbitant prices to private collectors. I sold him a hundred of them in a few weeks. He assured me that, given the prices he would offer for these drawings, a sum two to three times lower than the market price, they would never be resold but offered free of charge to his large foreign buyers, especially from Antwerp. I sold him two oil paintings by Miró, which he paid the equivalent of €700,000, as well as the Césars, at wholesale prices: the equivalent of €120,000 for the hundred drawings. The demand became pressing, so I transformed my living spaces into a manufacturing or storage workshop, but I was not at the end of my surprises.

One day, during a transaction in the Retelet gallery, I was leafing through exhibition catalogs and was greatly surprised to discover the famous aluminium metal compression that I had gone to look for in that end-of-the-world junkyard. The book in which it was found listed an exhibition of César's work that Retelet had organized in Belgium, his country of origin; he had therefore had works lent to him by various collectors in addition to his own. My rejected compression was prominently displayed in this catalog, simply mounted on a base and under Plexiglas with the annotation under the photo: private collection Ferrero gallery!

I still have the catalog. The work I was refused had been bought by a small second-hand dealer, who sold it for a fortune to the Ferrero gallery, which kept it as a masterpiece in its private collection! This gallery owner was Caesar's dealer and friend. This meant that the work had indeed been created by him. That day, I understood a lot about the underground arcanes of the art market... My creations, reproduced in the exhaustive catalogs, had become authentic works thanks to their manipulation. My creations, reproduced in the exhaustive catalogues, had become authentic works of art thanks to their manipulation. By passing through the hands of the big auction houses, through those of collectors and experts, my forgeries had become real.

14. My lawyer, Caesar and I [1990]

In 1990, I went to Barcelona to study Hispanic artists in galleries
and museums: Diego Rivera, Frida Kahlo, Roberto Matta Echaur-
ren, Francisco Clemente, El Greco, and Goya - especially his engravings, the series of "Caprices", "Disasters of War" and "Bullfighting".
I owned some of them, but I had the possibility of buying others
from a collector in Andorra. I had acquired these engravings in exchange for six works by César - *good deal*! I got these sculptures in
welded iron for almost nothing, while the three complete series of
Goya's works were worth the equivalent of 300,000 € on the international market... but I kept them to feed my collectionnite.

After having scoured all the trendy places in Barcelona, in the
company of friends, I go to the cradle of classicism: Italy. Perfect,
in theory, to rest from our Catalan *fiestas*... I visit the galleries that
are interested in contemporary and modern art. I offer them *deals*.
Indeed, I have many Caesars to place in order to buy other artists
to expand my collection. I already own hundreds of drawings,
gouaches, oils on canvas by Miró, César, Arman, as well as some
drawings by Picasso and especially young artists, Basquiat, Jeff
Koons, Julian Schnabel and Luciano Castelli. I photographed
them, *booked them*, insured them, hung them on the walls of my
flat-gallery in Paris or hid them from the tax authorities in my safe
in the Geneva free port.

It was then that I arrived in Florence, city of art, love and beauty. The city dazzles my soul and touches me deeply. As a result, I don't feel like playing the collector selling fakes. The fashion, the beauty and the grace of the girls we meet force us to forget why we came there. They draw us into this whirlwind of *dolce vita*, aestheticism, epicureanism, permissiveness and *love*. The libertinism of the trendy Italian parties keeps us there for a long time. There are so many pleasures to taste here, what a shock! Between two moments stolen from the party, I find the time to meet Fiorella, a gallery owner very interested in some of my fake-true works. Double project: professional, of course; but also, visibly, I do not leave the lady indifferent. She explains to me that her parents, rich industrialists from Turin, left her this magnificent gallery in the heart of Florence and a budget that I can imagine is substantial. On the walls hang all the greatest masters of the late twentieth century. I recognize four compressions of Fiat 500 that Caesar must have made in an Italian press and that Fiorella acquired for the equivalent of €100,000. Luciano Castelli and Andy Warhol are also represented, as well as Cindy Sherman thanks to large format photos with unique prints.

Fiorella is a talented and tasteful interlocutor. To begin our partnership, she commissioned me to produce ten drawings and three compressions of César. Four drawings, mixed techniques, "Centaurs", and six drawings of "Chickens". It is important to know that, for the master, the Centaur represented him - he had his face and an enormous tail - while the chickens represented his feminine fantasies.

The three "César" compressions are the ones I made in a press in Gennevilliers, in the suburbs of Paris, from obsolete blue mopeds. I had bought these two-wheelers for a pittance. They corresponded well to what César was pressing in the late 1970s. Once stripped of their tires and all the plastic parts, then pressed with dignity, these three wrecks had become three magnificent prisms where one could recognize these old Motobécanes, the brand name appearing partially on these works of art. I had signed them by hand: "César79". I tell Fiorella that these works come from exchanges between César and me, in return for the photographic work I had done for him, for his exhibition catalogs and posters. She takes my word for it... and she is not entirely wrong: it is partly true for some of these works.

From Paris, I send the works by UPS. As soon as I received them, she sent me a sweet note: she wanted to see me again as soon as I was available. She transfers to my account the equivalent of 120 000 € for all the works. In itself, it's not much, but I have a goal: that she can resell them at least twice as much - always think of a long term relationship. With the help of feelings and business, I will see Fiorella very often throughout Europe, at contemporary art fairs, but also at my home and at her home, in her Florentine mini-palace.

My relationship with César and his entourage was excellent. The works that I sold were even bought underhandedly by people close to a gallery close to César who did not distinguish between the master's creations and mine. However, no one could have guessed that, in the years to come, I was going to make his value explode by enriching a considerable number of protagonists in Europe, the United States and Asia. César himself created a lot and distributed his production to restaurants in Nice or to friends, for all sorts of reasons. He would get upset when he discovered that a drawing he had offered was being sold again; he would then cause a scandal, even claiming that they were not authentic!

Nevertheless, there comes a time when I must stop the Caesars. One afternoon in Nice, I sell fifteen drawings to a gallery owner for the equivalent of €30,000, less than half of what dealers such as the Ferrero gallery were selling them for. Two days later, I was alerted by my faithful lawyer, Gérard Baudoux. César went

14. My lawyer, Caesar and I [1990]

to his gallery owner, Ferrero, and he got angry when he saw many drawings, made by my hand, framed and hung in a prominent place in this gallery, authenticated and therefore around the equivalent of 5000 € each! A little calmed down, the master recognized that they were "of good quality" but, not remembering to have created them, he wrote on each drawing, in big and bold letters: "False". It remained for Caesar and Ferrero to elucidate the origin of the real certificates that accompanied them...

I can imagine the conflict that must have arisen between the greatest connoisseur and friend of Caesar and Caesar himself. Without my knowledge, I had created a schism. Since we had the same lawyer, Caesar let me know that he likes me, that my work is good enough not to insult him. However, if collectors learn that there are authenticated forgeries of Caesar on the art market, it could damage his steadily rising stock, cast doubt in people's minds and create immediate deflation.

Maître Baudoux tells me that neither César nor Ferrero will file a complaint. One to avoid spreading the scandal, the other because it was his son who had bought them from the secondhand dealer to sell them to his father! In return, I have to commit myself not to produce any more fake drawings of Caesar until his death! It goes without saying that I honored this agreement.

Well, almost.

15. How I saved Dario [1990]

As I am, I must constantly find other ways to sell my forgeries according to three strategies: by trading my creations for originals, by finding new ways to authenticate the works, and by renewing my sources of supply. Authentication and the origin of the collection is the key. Most of the value of a work is based on its provenance. This is its Ariadne's thread to the master. A family of billionaires, like the Fultons who sell their family jewels, is the guarantee of a royal peace to sell my fakes.

During a private party on the Croisette, I meet a colorful Argentinean. A joker, in his fifties and laughing, Dario seems very attracted to a friend, Bianca. He seems rich and lost; at my request, he is received with the greatest tenderness by Bianca, and we integrate him into our vicious circle. Without delay, we leave to take a big suite at the Martinez hotel, which we manage to book in a hurry at daybreak. We are seven, three boys and four girls. During two days, we turn over the suite and ourselves from top to bottom, without fearing to mix the kinds. Dario is very grateful for this. At the end of this party, he leaves us to return to his thirty-meter Italian boat anchored at Port Canto.

His *boat*, a Benetti, from the 1960s, is not great. It smells musty. On board, no service, not even a sailor: the yacht is a simple floating caravan, a poor vestige of a past lavish life. Perhaps Dario is not as rich as I imagined! Taking place in the guest cabin, we attack the vodka. While observing the cabin, I notice traces of unhooked works of art, replaced by coasters sheltering uninteresting nautical charts and photos, yellowed by time, of the ports where Dario has anchored his ship.

Dario is truly of ultra-rich extraction: his family owned property in Argentina, livestock and industry. He has been in exile since the dictators took power, looting, raping, appropriating without right or title everything that represented capitalism, blocking the bank accounts of the citizens and pushing the few survivors into exile. His family, very well known in Argentina, had wanted to stay and had been decimated while facing the army. Hence the *blues of* the fifty-year-old, who cries while telling me about his life. I comfort him. Struggling to come up with arguments to cheer him up, I pour him more vodka and change the conversation. So that his sorrow recedes, I speak to him about party, women, pleasures, the Benetti, our meeting and, fortuitously, about art, my passion. I feel that he needs to restore his reputation. I do not hide him my activity of forger. He is both surprised and interested by this unexpected information.

The man is at the end of his rope, and for good reason! Since his exile in the United States and then in Cannes, he has no news of his friends and relatives. Are they dead? Maybe, but not for sure. He himself fled, a few days before the junta came to power, saving his life by taking jewels, money, works of art of great value and French furniture. In Miami, he lived for five years, selling his diamonds, furniture, and works of art little by little, until he was almost broke; and today, here he is in front of me, flattened and, this time, completely out of money. He dreams of resurfacing, restoring his boat and taking his life in hand. But how? His boat is his only haven of peace. There was no way he could get rid of it. In any case, it is impossible to get a good price for it: the Benetti is too broken down!

I invite Dario to come to my house so that he can take a look at my collection of fakes just asking to become real by the usual magic. Once there, I show him the works in progress. He is interested. He was also amazed by my collection of fakes. He asked me if I had certificates of authenticity. I have some, but they are not very solid. So, Dario suggested that we make a story around what happened to his family in Argentina. We decide to give truth to my forgeries, by making Argentine documents. Their mission: to certify that my works come from the family collection. Dario provides me with the typewriter with the necessary Hispanic signs... and opens the South American market to me,

We create fake stamps from the Argentinean Customs and Justice Department and letterhead from Gallery 69, a Miami gallery that closed in 1985. We mix real and fake. In the political chaos of the time, we had an easy time sneaking my forgeries underneath authentic goods. So we combined photos of the works, official documents signed by an Argentine investigating judge, a restitution order stamped and signed by the Ministry of the Interior, all supported by documents from Argentine and American customs. This concerns a dozen fake paintings, representing the equivalent of one to two million euros. One of the documents mentions the order to the American authorities to seize in the Miami gallery the works that it had bought from Argentinean soldiers on the run in the United States. Around this letter, documents, purchase invoices and account books. Armed with such a file, Dario gave me an exclusive sales mandate to dispatch his works - mine, in fact.

This is how I was able to sell my forgeries to the largest galleries, foundations and auction houses, including Sotheby's, Phillip's and Christie's, as well as to discerning collectors. It was always the same channels. From this masterstroke, we made the equivalent of three million euros in a few months. I took the opportunity to sell the last remaining Miró, Chagall and Rivera paintings. We split the money. I deposited my share in a Swiss account and a new one in Luxembourg. I added to my collection by buying drawings by Picasso from private collections in France, Monaco and Miami. I also bought works by Yves Klein from the collection of James Baldwin in Saint-Paul.

Dario bailed out. I was happy about that. He had his yacht restored, and took the opportunity to settle in Mikonos where he opened... an art gallery that served me well afterwards.

16. My Michaux period [1991]

The biggest problem in this business? As with many trafficking operations, you have to control all the links in the network. You make so much money in a very short time that you are no longer suspicious of zealous intermediaries, those who are not good enough, who have not yet understood their interest in entering the scheme or who are jealous of you. I had already made a mistake of this type by sending my companion to sell some fake Dufy and Chagall to an unknown gallery owner. Apparently, I had not learned my lesson, since...

But let's start at the beginning, namely that I love Michaux. My nights of lack are haunted by his shadows. I still trace them, whether I hate the dark or carry it within me. They prevent me from living, from extending myself, from forgetting myself, from understanding. I want light, only white light, gold, red... I don't know anymore.

Henri Michaux worked under narcotics. He had tested mescaline, payotl and many other hallucinogens. His mind fertilized the inks. He let them flow, directing them by orienting the white sheet; and the inks unfolded, frozen black ghosts, shadows of the inside, dark spectres of the soul, black hallucination. Innumerable and irreducible were the spirits that inhabited him and that he rejected on the paper during his moments of lucidity.

I try to slide my black shadows in the manner of Michaux. After having built up a literature on his paintings, studied his writings and papers, I begin, on the floor of my room, to *attack* Michaux until I reach what I consider to be perfection. I work the inks-personnel-stains and the mescaline studies, feeding me of his works as *The knowledge by the chasms, emergence* resurgence or *The Space of the inside.* I am also fascinated by his life among the Tarahumara Indians, and I draw whole nights.

One day, Marino, a faithful friend if ever there was one, came to my studio. I had some inks soberly framed. I didn't know what to do with them as my walls were covered with works by Miró, Chagall, Max Ernst, young artists, but also with photographs. The whole thing was a visual mess. Above all, I was running out of cash, as the sign par excellence proved: my Porsche was out of gas. Coincidence or not, while browsing the advertisements of the regional newspaper, Mariano discovers that Philippe Rheims, an expert from Cannes, is looking for contemporary paintings to sell.

- Why don't you contact him?

No sooner said than done. We make an appointment, and here we are soon unloading our Michaux in front of the expert, who waits for us on the square of his house. Is the first look always the right one? The expert's eyes took in the pieces we were bringing him. There followed a discourse of expert and dealer which had only one objective: to make lower the price that I asked, that is to say the equivalent of fifteen thousand euros per work. As the production had not cost me much and had, on the other hand, allowed me to discover a new artist's universe, we found a common ground.

I signed the sale documents, and Marino and I left with the *cash.* Obviously, Rheims was happy; we were laughing our asses off. It was a light day, late spring. I learned later that the expert had sold my forgeries to a privileged adviser of François Mitterrand, former director of Air France, an important collector of

Henri Michaux's work. This gogo had bought them back at three or four times the price, as the law of the market dictates!

Three days later, the police knock on my door. After a quick search of my work space, I was taken away by two policemen. Once at the police station, I understood what had happened. The size of the paper I had used was a little larger than the same Canson used by Michaux in his time. I was in custody for a little extra inch in width and height. I should have faded the inks and then reduced them, but the rush had led me into a dead end. In this business, you have to be very vigilant and look at your work a thousand times. My inattention and these small centimeters were going to cost us eighteen months of reflection in the prison of Nice that I already knew too well... but which had been modernized, since 1985.

Nowadays, the reintegration structures offer the possibility of culture (library, art workshops, sports...) and especially of studying. I had studied art but I didn't have my baccalaureate. I had taken the beach option! This time, it was the opportunity to get that damn diploma. There were five candidates, including me: an Italian lawyer involved in a big drug deal, two gypsies who dealt in credit cards in large quantities, and a Portuguese mason. The courses were geography, history, English, Italian and French. We divided the tasks between us. The Italian did my Italian; I did the English and corrected the French essays. We all got the average. One hundred percent success rate: at the time, the Nice prison was among the best high schools in France.

My lawyer used this success to shorten my sentence by arguing to the judge: "Thanks to your structures, my client will finally be able to go to college in September. He wants to enroll in Art, Communication, Language. Eight days later I was free! Thanks to the baccalaureate, I had served seven months instead of eighteen. Well done, right?

17. My Moroccan period [1993]

After the affair of the false Chagall, Miró and Michaux, the galleries of the South of France and of Paris were reluctant to buy my real-false paintings. I had to leave to be forgotten... but where? To look for other companions, but who? Duly enrolled in Art, Communication, Language at the University of Nice, I went to live in Paris, rue Saint-Honoré, to think about the continuation of my life. At night, I zoned from the Marais to Beaubourg, finding a gloomy refuge where a fauna of *gays*, lesbians, heteros met, in a world lit with neon lights. The pallid faces reminded me of Goya's characters. Mine was diaphanous, translucent, giacometrical!

Spending most of my evenings in this underworld, I befriended Hicham, who was behind the bar. He is a trained stylist and has worked for some of the biggest names, but he wanted to create his own line.

As a good *bartender,* Hicham has a good sense of contact. He would later introduce me to gallery owners who came to his den looking for a je-ne-sais-quoi that they always found. In the meantime, one evening, he introduces me to a very beautiful princess with black eyes, *black star*, the star illuminating the bottom of her eyes, strong, dancing freely with a hypnotizing grace. Shy, I put a moment before approaching her, hoping that she would propose me. Soon, the love at first sight seizes us, she, oriental wonder and me, blackish character with the little avowable background.

Cïara-Ira came with sunshine in her luggage to continue her studies of surgery in an *American school*. Our powerful passion avoids us the dead times of the first meetings. The same evening, we spend the night at Cathy Guetta's at the Bains, where we stay until the morning to love each other, to get drunk of techno and classical history. I suggest her to come and sleep at the Louisiane but she prefers to take a cab and take me to her private hotel, in Neuilly. When I wake up, I have no memory of Cïara-Ira, of this evening, only details in my head in the form of a *puzzle*. My *black star* looks at me from every angle. She doesn't remember anything anymore! While getting dressed at high speed, she suggests me to go for a walk. This crossing of Neuilly to the street of the Seine allows us finally to know each other better. For six hours, we talked about everything, nothing, life, love, beauty, freedom, non-action in the most beautiful city in the world, that of lovers, that of Doisneau, that of existentialism - ours!

We arrive on the rue de Seine where I show him the galleries with which I have worked in the past. Not having any money left for the evening, I offer to wait for him for a moment. I run to change and pick up a dozen Chagalls, lithographs and gouaches, as well as a graphite drawing by Picasso on paper. I roll them up in a tube and run to sell them in a gallery at the bottom of the rue de Seine, near the docks. After fifteen minutes of negotiations, I cashed the equivalent of 150,000 €: 100,000 in checks and 50,000 in cash, which the gallery owner always keeps in his store for emergencies. I am aware that the prices offered are far from those of the market, but I don't care! In the end, I win. Then I still have three or four times that amount left in works rolled up in room #7 of the Louisiana. Leaving the gallery owner happy to have tricked me, I run like a headless rabbit to find my sweetheart. In less than an hour, I became rich again, able to offer my beautiful all that she can desire.

For my part, my only wish is that we stay together and transport ourselves on a Kilim carpet. Luckily, this wish is shared. We stay seconds, minutes, days, months at the Louisiane Hotel. We spend the time to love each other and to enjoy the Parisian life, its parties, its deliriums, without ceasing, until the sun of midday obliges us to cuddle us to better restart the following night. I take Cïara-Ira to art openings, exhibitions, artist visits. She loves it: instead of doing surgery, she wanted to study plastic arts. Her general of father preferred security. Frustration! I share with her what I know about art; she will use it later to become an art therapist in Paris.

I was introduced to his family, his sisters and brothers-in-law, as well as his doctor friends working in Paris. I was immediately adopted. I still love them. We find our rhythm. We go to Morocco six or eight times a year. Cïara-Ira makes me discover her country from top to bottom, from the society of power to the poverty and the various social injustices in place, at a time when Hassan II holds his people with an iron hand. I am introduced to the brother of the future king Mohamed VI, as well as to Moulay Rachid, the youngest prince. We travel all over Morocco, from Casablanca to Marrakech, from Essaouira to the Mamounia, in the desert, to see the sunrise that stretches to Algeria.

We decide to get married. Artists, our friends, Cïara-Ira's family living in Paris, mine and friends from all over Europe take part in our happiness. On this occasion, Christine, a gallery owner friend of mine on Avenue Matignon, absolutely wants me to meet Jean-Charles Villa, an American actor who wants to remake himself. His fortune was vaporized in parties, *coke* and prostitutes, until it led him to the meanders of precariousness. Knowing my lucrative activity of forger, he wished to meet me so that we make business with, in his sleeve, a major asset: his big network in the United States.

Back in Morocco, Cïara-Ira and I offer us a tour of contemporary artistic creation, including visual arts and music. We let ourselves be amazed by the country of the djinns, these malignant spirits which penetrate your spirit, bewitch you and try to make you crazy. To top it all off, Cïara-Ira becomes pregnant. We are in the angels.

At the Mamounia, where we stayed, I was surprised to be confronted with Modigliani, Dufy, Matisse, Derain, van Dongen and many others. They are crude and decorative fakes. In the great hall, it didn't do it at all! All these works were made by Réal Lessard, a forger of the *sixties* who had worked for the sulphurous Fernand Legros. The quality of what I have in front of me was closer to a *poster* than to a finished work. However, I learn that these copies sell for twenty thousand euros from time to time. A sad end for the man who was presented to me as "a genius of forgery"... On the brochure of the exhibition, this mediocre forger dares to write: "In a way, I complete the unfinished work of my predecessors. If Delacroix, Matisse, Marquet, Dufy, Van Dongen had been alive, they would have torn him apart alive!

Concerned about discretion, I do not substitute myself to their vengeful hand. Cïara-Ira wishes that we stay in the green, incognito, so that the pregnancy passes without stress and in optimal conditions. We intend to wait four or five months, the time to make sure that everything goes well, then leave for Miami for the birth of the baby. For love, I'm leaving my follies behind, moving away from the international art *business*, its pressures and its dangers. I don't feel I have the right to jeopardize our growing family. I have to question myself and look for new ways to use the market in practicing my art.

One day, the secretary of the Mamounia calls me because an email is waiting for me at the reception. Jean-Charles Villa, known as LøL, is telling me the story of a former semi star trained at the Cours Florent and then at the Actors Studio in New York. He insists on his address book: he can contact any actor, producer or director with whom he has made a film, but he also has connections in the *jet set* and the art world. In spite of myself, I am interested. Especially since he's playing on the heartstrings. According to him, I am the only one on this earth to restore his reputation, lost since his small roles in obscure films or, more recently, a dark film, *The Blackout*, where Claudia Schiffer, Beatrice Dalle, Dennis Hopper and Matthew Modine, the actor of *Birdy,* shone! Other *movies* completed his *underground.* All this smells like *blues* and the desire to be reborn; all this sounds right. I'm sending a message to LøL to tell him I'll meet him when I'm in Paris next.

Then I return to my real life of the moment. I find Cïara-Ira. We stroll in the gardens before going to an anthology party, organized by the youngest prince himself - certainly the most beautiful party I will attend in my whole life. I met Almodovar, behind his masks, and the inevitable Jean-Paul Gaultier, surrounded by his models. Cïara-Ira takes the head with Jamel Debbouze. Axl Rose and Billy Joel are *live.* We have a blast dancing the rock with Uma Thurman, dressed as a fairy, Naomi Campbell transformed into a voodoo princess, Tim Roth, Larry Gagosian and a very beautiful woman from the Fürstenberg family. Mickey Rourke, leaning on the edge of the stage, looks tetanized. Christie Turlington dances in her corner to the increasingly *fast* rhythms. I end up with the prince in the VIP area. We whistle champagne. I meet Princess Leila, her sisters and cousins. Their names escape me today, but I remember their beauty, their clothes and their laughter. My personal *queen* is radiant.

A few days later, it's a disaster. Leïla, Cïara-Ira's faithful friend and confidant, urges us to do ultrasounds in the gynecology department she runs at the Avicenne hospital in Rabat. On the screen, an inanimate embryo. At that moment, everything collapses; and

99

this is only the beginning. From sorrow to depression, from miscarriage to disillusionment, our fusion evaporates. The dream is over!

Our couple will have lasted one year and half. It will remain the most beautiful work that I will ever live. Thank you, my queen.

18. My Klein period [1994]

Alone in my *flat* since my return from Morocco, I contact Christine, my faithful flying gallery owner. I tell her about Jean-Charles Villa, specifying that he is harassing me by phone. At the bar of the Coste Hotel, she explains to me that she has helped LøL to position itself on the art market by introducing it to the *jet set of* collectors. By combining their address books, we should be able to contact billionaires *all over the world*! As a result, LøL started selling lithographs, drawings and gouaches by Chagall, Miró, Picasso and Matisse on behalf of Christine's gallery. An excellent salesman, he began to grow rich, *step by step, with* Christine, who entrusted him with more and more important works: Bernard Venet, Yves Klein, Georges Braque, as well as other recognized and more conceptual artists. Christine spoke to him about my work and, of course, let him imagine the much greater gains he could make with me.

Encouraged by this *pedigree*, I ask Christine to call Jean-Charles so we can talk *business*. The appointment takes place at my home, rue Saint-Honoré. Still in the *dark*, depressed, bereaved by this child I will never see but of which I keep the ultrasounds, the only memories of a lost hope, I want to go forward and retrace the dark path of life. LøL arrives at the appointment with another colorful character, Pat Veinard, former gallery owner in Monaco and art broker. They enter my *flat-gallery* and are stunned by the quality and the number of works that are there. And this is only the tip of the *art iceberg*: the rest is in the land of the Helvetians! In addition to my fake Kleins, Chagalls and Légers, my collection includes genuine, authenticated and recognized works that I bought with the money from the looting of the Fulton and Gould estates.

Impressed, LøL and Pat sit on my sofa designed by the interior designer Cassina in the 1960s. The two fellows, more interested in money than in the love of art, make me a very direct proposal. They want to buy everything from me, or at least get my collection back in some way. They know I'm *down* and think, wrongly, that I don't care about what adorns my home, including the sculptures of Rodin, Arman, César, including my five post-cubist Picassos, my little Rembrandt, the Warhol "Marilyn Monroe", including the portrait that the latter has drawn of me.

Pat Veinard explains that he has direct access to the Klein and César families, which is worth its weight in gold. As far as Yves Klein is concerned, he knows very well the expert Daniel Moquay and Rotraut Klein, the master's widow, who hold the creative capital of the work with an iron hand. As for César, he claims to be close to Alain-Dominique Perrin, his patron, and his companion, Stéphanie Busuttil. He adds:

- Provide me with photos of the works you want to authenticate, and I will show them to the rightful owners. Only when they see them, they will affix an archive number, the detailed certificate of the work, the stamp and the signature of the master on the back of each one.

LøL explains that he will take care of selling the works throughout Europe, once the certificates of authenticity have been drawn up. I cut short César: I had made a commitment to the master, we had the same lawyer, I didn't want any trouble... and it was only a matter of time. On the other hand, I accepted the *deal* for Klein, as it was so perilous to pass on the works of this master without a pass.

I offer to sell Klein's to them, provided that I retain full control over what is sold, to whom and at what price. I offer them 30% of the sale price, which would itself be 40-50% below the master's price, so that our buyers can make a nice profit by reselling them to their wealthy clients. As for me, I would receive 70% of the value of the works sold. They accept my proposal.

So I set to work. I try to understand the mixture that made up his famous blue, the one called "Klein blue". I buy a dozen real sea sponges fished in Israel. Untreated, full of sand and pieces of shells, they are raw. Their shapes are bizarre, some with big holes and deep asperities. I also buy catalogs of public sales, in a large bookshop in Saint-Germain, in the one of the Museum of Modern Art in Nice and, through my friends, at Christie's and Sotheby's. There I found the photos and prices of Klein's works sold recently. Last challenge: to find the formula for ultramarine blue.

I found it at M. Sennelier's, a great dealer in colors and pigments on the Quai Voltaire. As a regular customer, I explain to him that I have to restore some sponges by Yves Klein which, with time, have become lighter. He is not fooled: all of Paris knows that I am a counterfeiter. Nevertheless, he explains to me exactly what I have to buy, a powder pigment, dark ultramarine blue, another light ultramarine blue, and a last one, pink, to be used sparingly. It's up to me to figure out how to mix and bind them with the bronzer, a kind of transparent resin sold by the liter. I buy the ingredients for the magic potion, as well as brushes, an airbrush, a compressor, and I go into action.

After many tests on Canson sheets, I find the right proportions and notice that the result dries very quickly. I observe my sponges, the real ones, their mounting on rusty threaded steel rods. I learn from books that some bases are large stones found in gardens, only on the French Riviera. On the heights of Grasse, I rent a small villa-workshop and I collect several stones. I have the stems made by

18. My Klein period [1994]

an iron worker. He cut me a dozen of them, rusty, to the diameter and length that I indicated to him. He bends some of them for me, because none of these rods must look like the others. I bring him the stones I have collected so that he can drill them to force the concrete rods in. Indeed, everything must fit without glue.

I polish the base of these pedestals so that they are flat, and the balance of the sponge sculptures is perfect. Klein, a black belt in judo, had a sense of balance! Then, with a chisel, I rework the sponges. In a bucket, I put water and fast-setting plaster. The mixture seems to be ready, so I dip my sponges in it and they immediately become hard when, three hours later, they are dry. Once hardened and dry, I put them on their steel rod. I use the mixtures of pigments and bronzer to paint these animals with a brush. In the sun and outdoors, it dries quickly, and I can do several coats without delay.

The most tedious part remains: injecting the color that I can't apply with a brush into the gaps and holes, using large syringes. Again, I let it dry and then I finish my work with the airbrush to unify these fakes. A few hours later, I am happy with the result. The spirit of Yves Klein is respected from A to Z. The blue, applied differently on the sponges, gives them the right reflections. Above all, fixed with bronzer, my pieces have the velvety aspect required. The Klein catalog has just been enriched with ten new sculptures.

I keep four of them for myself, including a pink one, and I deliver the other six to my sponsors. The intermediary is essential, because I know that Klein's heirs have had their eye on me since I was in prison and that the newspapers have been spreading rumors and gossip about me. My accomplice friends obtained the expert reports, confirmed as they should be on the back of the photos of each sculpture. My forgeries are now real!

I don't want the new Kleins to be sold in Paris or even in France. Therefore, I let LøL sell them, below the market price, to a client in Seoul who bought two of them for the equivalent of €120,000 each, transferred to my Luxembourg account. The four others were sold at about the same price, one to a collector in London, one to Monaco and two to a gallery owner in Copenhagen. None of the sponges, none of the bases were signed Y. K. nor dated... except for my pink sculpture which I signed in black felt pen, on the back, in small, Y. K. 61.

Once again, I won my bet, finding new clients and making a turnover of about 600,000 € - on the two Copenhagen sales, I had to give a discount at the insistence of my buyers. Of course, the public sales catalogs suggested higher prices, but so what? Between materials and miscellaneous expenses, I spent, like Klein in 1960, very little: barely the equivalent of 5,000 €. In exchange, I did some exciting work and successfully took on a new challenge. Frankly, the discount was not important.

Much later, in a gallery on the rue des Beaux-arts in Paris, I saw a blue sponge, a little light. I entered, asked to touch it and asked about its selling price. A very beautiful woman announced to me, with a smile to die for: 300 000 euros.

- Wow, it's expensive, I answer him.

- I know, but his owner doesn't want to lower the price; and he is stubborn, Stéphane Collaro!

19. The burial of Caesar
[10 December 1998]

Thursday, December 10, 1998, Paris, Montparnasse cemetery. Two steps away from Baudelaire's tomb, in a landscape of frost, César's friends and relatives accompany the artist to his final resting place. Behind the tears and dignity, a muted war is brewing. At stake: the master's inheritance, several tens of millions of euros.

In fact, I am the only one to pay a personal tribute, in all discretion, to the master whom I have loved and copied without betraying him. I see Rosine and Anna Baldaccini, César's wife and daughter, as well as Stéphanie Busuttil, his last companion and beneficiary, on the arm of Alain-Dominique Perrin, the executor of his will. In 1990, the latter, CEO of the powerful house of Cartier, had introduced Stéphanie to the master, who was then at the height of his fame. She was only nineteen years old, César could be her grandfather. The meeting with César led her to play an ambiguous role. She was at the same time mistress and secretary, then nurse and business manager when the artist, undermined by a lightning cancer found himself confined to a hospital bed. The beautiful Stephanie is, by will, the owner of the artist's moral rights. This allows her to authenticate the master's creations. I will wait two days before placing on the grave a small compression of cardboard boxes that contained flowers.

The imbroglio surrounding his succession lasted nearly fifteen years! The wills distributing the fortune did not have time to be drawn up, and the master left behind a legal chaos. The tax authorities blocked the file for a long time. The tax authorities could not calculate the amount of the inheritance tax with certainty. And for good reason: many works were missing from the inventory! The gendarmes of the Marseille Research Section, who investigated the disappearance of a large quantity of specimens, concluded that at least 350 works had disappeared from the workshop and the foundry. It was Rosine and Anna Baldaccini who alerted the tax authorities. In 2002, Bercy demanded a phenomenal adjustment of 38 million euros. It must be said that the explanations of the moral right holder were quite surprising.

For example, when the gendarmes heard Stephanie Busuttil on the disappearance of *Poule à limes in wood and iron, ca.* 1970, a sculpture of almost one meter high and of great artistic and historical value, answer:

- I had this work destroyed.

We laugh! However, it was discovered that many works were indeed broken by Caesar's foundry in the days following his death. Well informed, the tax authorities also searched for a *black Citroën ZX* that had been exhibited in Venice in 1995. This one has the particularity of being the only one to have the steering wheel on the right. How could this work have slipped away? Other major works were missing, such as *L'Improvisation*, representing a welded character in 1984, or *L'Insecte africain* of 1982 which had conveniently flown away...

Maître Guilloteau, one of Stéphanie's lawyers, put forward a justification that was, to say the least, far-fetched:

- César worked a lot on his works by modifying them or having them modified; some sculptures were transformed and became new pieces.

What a joke!

To strengthen her defense on the possible inheritance tax to be paid in dation, that is to say by giving works, Stéphanie Busuttil has surrounded herself with Maître Belot, the lawyer involved in the affair of the sulphurous video-tape of Jean-Claude Méry. The lawyer wished to assert the rights of the beneficiary on the civil society of the workshop César, the SCAC, constituted in 1997, and that Stéphanie controlled partly. The other part of the Baldaccini family was also suspended on the results of the tax investigation.

The bitter battle between Anna Baldiccini and Stéphanie Busuttil led the latter to try to have the twenty-two awards seized on the eve of the César awards ceremony on February 21, 2001. The reason: forgery and use of forgeries. The argument: the statuettes would have been realized by a "sur moulage" on an old bronze, which would flout the right of the sculptor. In reality, Anna Baldaccini had the trophies made from the original belonging to Georges Cravenne, secretary general of the Academy of Arts and Techniques of Cinema, friend of the sculptor and founder of the César ceremony. However, to complicate the case, the justice system discovered that another founder had also been solicited, with whom a hundred undeclared works were stagnating. Adding color to this battle, false documents were also added to the file. Among them was a copy of an agreement signed between Georges Cravenne and César according to which César made a gift of this original to his friend, according to Didier Benheim, lawyer for the sculptor. In response, the Court of Appeal has long put under guardianship the assets of Stephanie Busuttil. Alain-Dominique Perrin, the family friend, who made himself indispensable to the sculptor, played an active role in this affair; he is indeed the executor of Caesar's will and must, as such, ensure that the last wishes of the master are respected and that the inheritance is properly distributed.

If Caesar can reconsider things from above, I don't know if he cries or laughs, but one thing is certain: he must not *rest in peace*. For me, this imbroglio was good news: it made it much easier to "pursue the work of the master" freely and en masse. Some works had disappeared? Others were destroyed? Let's add forgeries to maximize Caesar's glory! It is in this context that I provoked a meeting at home with my two companions, LøL and Pat. I proposed to them to sell my Caesars. I had about thirty of them: compressions of 750 Honda motorcycles from 1975, silver cutlery, Coca-Cola cans, drawings of chickens, centaurs, "homage to Morandi" that I had made by crushing enamel coffee pots and gluing them on large white panels, framed in Plexiglas and signed César. To complete the lot, I also had to offer some rusted and compressed children's pedal cars. They were of good provenance but were neither listed in the exhaustive catalog of the master's work, nor authenticated by his rightful owner, the young widow, or by the executor of his estate. Pat promised me that he would take care of it.

I validated the project on the condition that the business be done quietly, and especially that I not appear. My two associates left with some photos I had taken with my digital Leica. I had photographed two motorcycle compressions from the 1970s, two Elnet lacquer cans from the 1980s, and a Coca-Cola compression. All of these works were signed by the master.

While waiting for the result, I adopted the very *British* attitude of "wait and see": it was our first case concerning César. My brother Franck was very suspicious when he heard about this new project. He offered to take my place in cashing in the profits of the business. That suited me. While I was at it, I asked him to transport the stocks... and suggested to make fakes: nothing could be easier

- anyone can make them! I also got Yaël Marciano, a trusted friend and party-goer, a former model, *tennis player* and *playboy*, who had become a powerhouse of Parisian nights.

Two days later, LøL and Pat contacted me by *e-mail*. They had the certificates for the five cuts and, with them, the buyers who were waiting for them. I told them that my brother would deal with them. They made an appointment to come and pick up the five prints and paid Frank the equivalent of €60,000. They had sold all these works to a gallery owner in Antwerp who had come specially to Paris to take possession of them. Franck collected the money in *cash* and put it in an account in Luxembourg.

That's how LøL and Yaël became my salesmen. Pat was the magician of expertises; and my brother, my assistant in charge of making hundreds of other compressions, drawings, homage to Morandi, which took the same path, generating uncommon profits. Franck also photographed thirty-three drawings of chickens and centaurs signed by César, ten compressions of metal, toys, small cars - César loved cars, he crushed them! - as well as six "Tributes to Morandi" made in his studio. The total price Franck asked for the drawings was 50,000 €. This was more than reasonable, at €1500 per drawing... which Cesar sold for three times that amount. For the ten compressions of metal objects purchased at once, Franck demanded €200,000. As for the superb "Tributes to Morandi", all it took was €75,000 to buy them, whereas they were worth three times that amount on the market. LøL negotiated the lot for the equivalent of €250,000. The idea that we were starting to negotiate the price of our creations bothered me, but since they were buying in large quantities, I agreed with Franck, provided that it was in *cash*. The money would go to another account, in another bank, always in Luxembourg, for a simple reason: the Luxembourg law could, on international tax rogatory commission, ask the banking system of the Grand Duchy of Luxembourg to give information on the payments made by a private individual, but only on a bank. Knowing this, we had opened accounts in eight different banks. In France, if you have accounts in several banks, the Bank of France informs the tax inspectors about all the accounts; in Luxembourg, at least at that time, this does not exist!

A week later, LøL and Pat come to pick up the works that Franck has offered them, with a small truck and a huge envelope containing the promised *cash.*

I was bluffed by the efficiency of LøL and Pat. Thanks to them, I was lulled by the soft sound of the thirty-ton metal presses crushing all sorts of objects without interruption to feed the industry of the master's forgeries. LøL, Pat and Yael were my total screen, and I enjoyed it. With my brother, I could concentrate on the creation, in the most opaque shadow; they were selling the stuff! We became a team of forgers where each one had his role to hold and knew the price of discretion to respect; and the good news for this flourishing *business*, it is that the Asian market opened: the Japanese and Chinese customers were asking for more...

20. My Japanese period [1999]

In 1999, I left alone for Japan. I know nothing about this country. The only thing I know for sure is that its literature - its theater in particular - and especially its cinema fascinate me. I bring with me three Picassos (oil on canvas from 1930 to 1942), about thirty drawings by César and two compressions of hair spray. Beforehand, I emailed my prospects the photos of the works, their size and price. In exchange, I received an interesting offer from the Nippon Art Exchange Gallery, and I decided, for this time, to do without an intermediary. An appointment was made at the Island Shangri-La Hotel to finalize the transaction, after the usual checks on authenticity and provenance.

I declare to customs that these pieces belong to one of my companies. All the Caesars are certified by the artist's widow. The Picassos are part of my collection and are all real - I had bought them with part of the Tel Aviv funds. The money from this transaction was transferred from a Japanese bank to the Fortis Bank in Brussels, to the account of one of my companies.

Once at the hotel, the negotiations begin. Slowly. Sake after sake, my buyers spend the whole day playing with my nerves by diverting the conversations, changing constantly the subject to try to break the prices. They are smart! They have the power and the time to wear me down; but they like the works, I can feel it. They leave the Island Shangri-La without us having finalized our transaction. Appointment is made for the next day, same time. I am anxious at the idea of all this time still to lose to support them. In this art business, you have to think rich, look rich, but look poor and uneducated. In terms of money, confidence is a utopia. For the rest, I like to look like a fool. On this session, I am aware that I was scanned from top to bottom. My nervousness did not escape my interlocutors, who obviously took advantage of it.

Six hours after we resumed our talks, exhausted and drunk from drinking too much sake to calm down, I agreed to sell the Picassos for $850,000. Obviously, it is worth more. They are superb, appraised and archived. They would have sold for fifty percent more at public auction. Nevertheless, I made two and a half times my purchase price. We parted as good friends (you bet) and knew we had made a great *deal*. They ask if I own any more. The truth is that I do, but not for them! I leave with my thirty drawings of César - proof that, decidedly, the Japanese market is not ready for this master - and the two prints, my interlocutors not being interested. I arrive too early. Taking advantage of my escapade, I take the pulse of the Japanese creation. I wander in the avant-garde galleries, like Tamenaga and Art gallery. I look at what the designers are up to and almost devour Watanabe's *showroom*, as a convulsive *addict of* Japanese fashion.

In the aftermath, I spend long hours in the *corner of* Yohji Yamamoto, my favorite designer: in Paris, I am already a privileged client of this artist-architect with a rare *look*. I fell in love with his latest Japanese collection, since Yamamoto does not offer the same lines in Tokyo, Paris or London: each country has its exclusivities.

In the various galleries, I buy rare prints by Hasegawa, the greatest Japanese printmaker using the black manner, much sought after in Europe and the United States. On my return, I hang them next to two Zao Wou-Ki oil paintings, *ca.* 1950. The Japanese space of my *flat-gallery* serves as a refuge for me, but I must admit the obvious: I am surrounded by art and empty of life!

During my stay in Tokyo, Franck made eight new tributes to Morandi in his studio. Then he went to Grasse to compress about fifty Cesarean works: old blue mopeds from the 1970s, old water heater interiors found on the spot and already compressed, as well as little children's pedal cars from the 1950s that he had found at the Clignancourt and Saint-Ouen flea markets. At a wholesaler in Cannes for kitchen equipment for large restaurants, he bought ladles, strainers, whisks, long-bladed knives... in short, everything that can be compressed. In Grasse hypermarkets, he also bought pallets of Coca-Cola cans, emptying the contents into the gutter. At the scrap yard, he recovered old aluminum cans that had contained perfume bases and essences. Finally, he brought down to Grasse old wristwatches and gussets collected in large quantities; once compressed into a perfect prism, these antiques would remain frozen in an indefinite space of time, for all eternity, indicating all the time zones, all the hours of light and shadow over the last thirty years! *Fun,* this mixed time, crushed, stopped in its tracks... But the *business does* not stop at our workshops: knowing that we are big customers, the second-hand dealers wait for us every week. They don't know the purpose of our business, and they wonder if we make substantial profits, so they calculate the price of the pieces we pay them in *cash* without negotiating.

Back from Japan, my mission was to control Franck's work and then sign "César" on all the art pieces. The most tedious part, once the Coke cans had been compressed? Using a dentist's grinder to remove the bar codes that appeared on the prism. I was also careful to use acid to soften the bright red color by washing it away so that it would be representative of the 1980s. Same precaution for the new aluminum and stainless steel material. Then, and only then, I take the necessary pictures for the certificates complacently delivered by Caesar's widow thanks to Pat's intervention.

I am aware that, at the speed at which we are putting our works on the international market, we risk saturating it to the point of lowering the value of the César awards, real or fake. We have to avoid the *warnings going off.* So we decide to stop the sales for a few weeks. LøL and Pat are furious. They want to take advantage of the mess surrounding the César estate to sell works in large quantities. Distrustful, I prefer to wait; conciliatory, I promise them that they will have new works soon. Patience and length of time, etc.

21. My Chinese Period [1999]

One day, late in the afternoon, Yohji calls me. He is with Kimiko, a stylist from Shanghai, and a certain Koji, a cultural attaché to the Chinese government. I received them at my home without salamalecs; I am not inclined to sophisticated civility.

Kimiko enters first, taking off her shoes, a *book* in her arms. She is not pretty, but she is a brilliant stylist. Koji and Yohji follow, respecting the same ritual. I leave them both in the *flat* to stay with Kimiko. Sitting on the floor, she shows me her stylistic creations that I find very banal. After a few uninteresting remarks, I try to orient her towards Shanghai, the local creation, the possible openings, etc. When the other two come back to us, I feel that they are more impressed by the quantity of works that cover my walls than by their quality. They are no more impressed than that by the pieces piled up against each other, by the Rodin sculptures I bought with the money from the fake Caesars, even by authentic Picasso drawings and oils from the 1950s. In the bric-a-brac of my collection, an impressive quantity of Caesars, sculptures and drawings already signed by me, were waiting for their certificate of authenticity, surrounded by works of friendly artists, plastic creators in precariousness, that I tried to bring out of the shadows by buying them without discussing their price.

These works by strangers were placed here and there, a little because I had no other place, a lot so that they could be seen by the art professionals who visited me. Inspecting this maelstrom, Kimiko took in her hands Jeff Koons' *Rabbit* in chromed aluminum, a piece I got for ten unauthenticated Caesar's compressions... and which I would never sell. At that time, it was already worth two million dollars!

Neither Kimiko, nor Yohji, nor Koji are shocked at the sight of my two *trash-porn* sculptures of Jake and Dinos Chapman, bought at the Saatchi Gallery in London. However, one of the sculptures represents quadruplets connected by the head. At the top of these heads, each facing a different direction, is a common anus, surely intended to evacuate their bad thoughts and the horror of this life. My Asian friends thought this work was great.

The second Chapman sculpture still represents a child, always in the same material, always with an outrageous make-up, the hallucinated fixed look and extended by long false eyelashes. Unlike the quadricéphales, he is provided with a long, black and wavy wig that falls on his shoulders, androgynous - look. His arms and his chest are covered with a short-sleeved T-shirt bearing the inscription "no sex". His feet covered with Nike socks were also shod with small black Nike; his *shorts*, lowered, discovered a woman's sex from which emerges a turgid boy's sex. This so simple sculpture dazzled me. The concept, the allegory, the *no-sex*, the self-sufficiency are expressed with a sophisticated and raw realism! My visitors are interested in my collection of Araki's photos - his black and white nudes, waxed, bound, *bondage* - and my original Newton prints, in this case the photos of two naked bimbos having a blast in the back of a limousine. On the other hand, no interest for the photo, though taken by Annie Leibovitz, immortalizing Mick Jagger in full concert, sweating, jumping, bare-chested on stage. No more passion for the other photos, even the one by Mapplethorpe, a single black and white print on platinum paper, which represents a naked black man, crouching, his head in his lap revealing his shaven head. This shot, taken against the light, shows his sex hanging down, huge and long, almost touching the ground, a reptilian fantasy of a boa between his legs.

My visitors are mostly interested in my Zao Wou-Ki and eight rare prints by the Japanese master Hasegawa, including the famous "black manners", works from different periods that I brought back from Tokyo and that I have owned for quite some time. We negotiate in the Japanese way, leaving time to time.

Koji and Kimiko can't take it anymore: they remain glued in front of the Araki. These tortured and decadent pleasures are incomprehensible to the uninformed *Frenchy*. Fortunately, the Asians, freed from our European-American puritanism, have a different outlook on love, life and sex. Since Mishima, Japanese art has never stopped moving forward without taboos and, long before him, the ancestral *sex attitude*. Nevertheless, it is out of the question that I give up my Araki; I had tracked down unceasingly the various exhibitions where I bought the *hardest* therefore the most representative photos of the master Araki illustrating the untouchable, the rare, *explosive-chronic-sex*. After a long reflection, Yohji, proposes me to exchange some of my works against some of his, glimpsed during the *after* parade reception he gave at his place. He knows that, like him, I am attached to the pieces I own. As best he can, he tells me of his interest in two Hasegawa anthologies, two very large and recent Zao Wou-Ki... and a Picasso from the 1950s, a post-cubist oil on canvas that is fake but listed as real. I don't want to sell him this creation. But, in fact, he is interested in almost everything. Indeed, he also wants one of the two Chapmans and two sculptures by César, freshly compressed by Franck, representing prisms of intertwined, very graphic, copper faucet pipes.

I don't want to admit that there is nothing in his collection that interests me. So I offered to sell him a very large Zao Wou-Ki for $500,000, especially since I didn't have the space to hang it decently. In the same breath, I agreed to sell him the two Hasegawa prints from the 1930s for $45,000, as well as the two Caesars for $50,000, for which I promised certificates within 48 hours. A shrewd negotiator, he offered me $550,000 for the whole, 60% by bank transfer to my company account in Brussels and a 40% credit note on his creations, as a preview. He will have the works delivered directly to Tokyo by Chenus, a specialist in the transport of works of art. I know I will miss my great Zao Wou-Ki of 1987: he expresses the strength, the finesse of red, green, blue, yellow colors, white star spaces, black impressions, whipped spots, gestured away by his powerful gesture. What a brilliant gesture! Realistic abstraction of his inner world, intuitive, spontaneous expression of the greatest contemporary Chinese artist living and working in Paris for four or five decades. But art must circulate, pleasure too.

I am surprised by Yohji's bulimia for visual art. I only know him through his work as a designer and his advanced conceptual visions. I will remain faithful to Junya Watanabe and therefore to "Comme des garçons".

Koji and Kimiko wait while Yohji and I negotiate. Afterwards, they make me a very pleasant proposal. They are looking for a curator to promote young Chinese artists living mainly in Shanghai. They need someone who can introduce these unknowns to the Western world. Me, for example. The opening up of a country like China starts with its culture, the rest will follow. Their project is to bring out of total anonymity its creators, to target them, to define the different artistic currents and to make them tour in international exhibitions. On the program: writing of books, mediatization and communication with the specialized media. Quite a proposal!

Back home, Koji and Kimiko send me a lot of items from China and Shanghai. I am preparing to leave once my current *business* worries are settled: I want to arrive with complete freedom of action.

22. My LøL period [1999]

Jean-Charles Villa invites me to his apartment on rue des Petits-Champs, where he lives with Pamela Anglade, the actor's ex-wife. Pat is there too. LøL wants to show me a "Tribute to Morandi". On a whitewashed panel, like the ones Franck makes, he has glued vertically two enamel coffee pots, one green and one red, after crushing them and spreading the enamel on the background. My verdict is formal: this thing has nothing to do with a Caesar. The background is too white; the enamel colors are not blended, creating a line of demarcation between the two coffee pots. If they had been made on two separate panels, we would have been closer to the mark! I am appalled. This guy has no talent and risks putting up for sale works that dishonor the spirit of the master. He asks me to imitate Caesar's signature because he doesn't know how to do it. He promises me that this work will only serve to decorate his apartment. I explain to him that, even signed, this thing is unsaleable. If he ever tries his luck, he shoots us. With these precautions in place, against my will, I sign this piece of junk that I would not have wanted in my apartment and that would have been better called *Déshommage à Morandi*.

After that, LøL pays me for the fifty or so compressions and the eight "Homage to Morandi" - perfectly Caesar-like - that Franck had made a few weeks earlier, in the land saturated with unbearable smells where magicians transform scrap metal into works of art, and then our accounts into gold. For my part, I propose to sell fifteen more compressions and eight new "Homage to Morandi", applying the drip strategy. I didn't want to tell Pat and my host how many similar works we had in store. They would have liked to market all the works immediately! I demanded the equivalent of €300,000 for the compressions and €80,000 for the eight "Tribute to Morandi" works, a handsome sum for these works, which came to €4,500 including transport.

Out of the 380,000 € I ask for, my dealers offer me 300,000: their profit margin is too tight, the risks are great, etc. I play the ulcerated and let them believe that we might not close this deal. I play the ulcerated and let them believe that we might not close this deal. Japanese style, I let the negotiation drag on. I have a hunch that I should not let them get the upper hand on my brother and me, nor allow them to devalue our work by negotiating it so low. As a bonus, I try to make them doubt me, in case they think they are the only ones selling our creations. These naïve people don't know my *background*, nor my talent to convince the biggest collectors to buy or trade me my Caesars for real works by *pop artist* Tom Wesselmann or Arman, for example. I let them simmer in vibrate mode, then I play the game of the uptight guy. So I accept their offer on condition that I get paid within 48 hours and in *cash*. I will give them the works on the day of payment.

Two days have not passed when LøL rings my doorbell. He is accompanied by Pat and movers to take the pieces away in a small truck. He gives me the agreed amount in cash. Pat and the art workers pack up my Caesars. Inwardly, I laugh to see how delicately they handle them, as if they were holding Monet's fragile *Water Lilies* in their hands, even though these objects have been compressed under dozens of tons and are in no danger of breaking!

However, a bad surprise awaits my accomplices. Indeed, I take advantage of this exchange to specify to LøL that I stop, for an undetermined moment, the sale of the César. My argument: at the rate we are feeding him, the French and European markets are about to be saturated. When he asks me what makes me think that, I explain that I see the works I sold them everywhere - in the galleries on the Rue de Seine, in those on the Avenue Matignon, in the catalogs of public sales, and even on the web pages of a gallery in Flanders. I would add that the prices I have noted are on average six times higher than those I have sold to them. LøL and Pat look vaguely upset, but nothing more. Strange!

Franck transports the money by train to Geneva. Before opening an account at the UBS, he creates a company *through* a fiduciary. In the Financial Art Exchange, neither my name nor that of my brother appears. Simply, in a safe deposit box of this bank, we have 99% of the shares of this new company. Bearer shares! Numbered account! *Security* above all! However, I feel like I'm slipping into a nasty spiral. A trap is sucking me in, I can feel it, but I no longer have a precise reference point. Everything seems to me blurred.

What is space? The light? The *dark*? The shape? The beauty? The full? Emptiness? The real? The false? The work and its limit? These questions are mixed up in my mind. I lose myself by living in the triangle of love, sex and art. And then, nobody or almost nobody has any reservations about this mass of fake and real works that I flood the international market with. So, why worry?

23. My clash period [End 1999]

At the end of 1999, that's all anyone talks about: the changeover from the franc to the euro. A memorable *one-shot* and a major headache for the art world! Millions of francs in *cash* plus the astronomical profits that gallery owners were making seemed to be safe from the (not very fine) taxmen!

Some galleries are financed by thugs, occult owners of nightclubs or gambling circles, bank robbers, pure Colombian wholesalers, racketeers and pimps. These gangs hand over fortunes in millions of francs, in *cash*, to the gallery owner who takes care of laundering this manna by buying works of art from us that he resells with big profits. As players in this game of fools, we in turn launder all this money, which saves the holders of these criminal fortunes from going to the Bank of France, in 2002, to exchange them for containers. We are the ones who make the money disappear abroad, in our *paradises*. No wonder that some "investors" put at the disposal of some artists one or two millions in *cash* for their next works!

The proximity of this changeover to the euro explains in part the eagerness of buyers to buy our Caesars, paid in *cash* and taken directly from my *flat-gallery*. Thus, I find myself at the heart of the scheme. No one wants to take the risks, even me. The game is too profitable. Our "gang of counterfeiters", as the press calls us, washes the equivalent of twenty million euros in less than five years, according to the financial cops.

The peak of this colossal washing machine? The Foire Internationale d'Art Contemporain de Paris - the famous FIAC which, at the time, was held at the Porte de Versailles. *Dressed in* an *arty fashion*, I went with Franck to the inauguration. Not a TV, not a specialized magazine is missing. The cameramen feast their eyes on the hundreds of booths ultra supplied with pieces of great international artists, dead or alive. I try to avoid taking pictures but I stop, glass of champagne in hand, at some key stands, including the one of the Guy Pieters gallery. In passing, I meet again gallery owners from the rue de Seine like Laurent Strouck and Anne Lettrée. Many don't know who I am anymore.

On Guy Pieters' stand, I see a lot of works that Franck and I made a few months earlier. They are for sale at prices that make you dizzy: the equivalent of €150,000 for a "Tribute to Morandi" (there are twelve on the stand!), the equivalent of €100,000 to €400,000 for our compressions! I am levitating, but Franck is white-green with rage. He has just seen other works that are less Caesar-like than ours, and at equivalent prices. In my turn, I observe the stall. I, who know Caesar's work by heart, see the obvious: there is not a single one that the master has done, and... My eyes widen. LøL has indeed put up for sale the *Déshommage à Morandi*, dated "*circa* 1970" and certified by the César workshop. You can buy this filth for the equivalent of 45 000 €, on the stand of the Pieters gallery! The deceit of my sidekick reaches me in the depths of my being. This failed work is on the walls of the most important gallery in Europe dealing with *pop art* and New Realism! Total delirium!

I call a cab and take Franck, as disgusted as me. Direction rue des Petits Champs. I announce to Pamela that we are in the vicinity. She invites me to pass but specifies that she is alone. I ask anyway the driver to go to 91, rue Saint-Honoré; I take my colt 11,43 of 1921; I supply the magazine; and, in the cab, I sniff a gram of coke in a line. I am boosted.

Pamela, happy to see me again, asks me lots of questions about my "Shanghai *trip*" while doing her *star* and drawing on her mirror white lines of about ten grams. We talk about everything and especially about nothing. My caliber is itching. I hope for the arrival of LøL and Pat. Around me, a considerable number of false Caesars, some still in progress, compressions, drawings, not finished and not Caesar-like for a penny, and a hundred "things" in progress!

No doubt about it, LøL cheated me big time! If you add to his fakes the works I was working on, plus my stock reserved for LøL and Pat for a parsimonious *dispatching*, we were burning up the market. I am appalled and can hardly think.

My first idea: when LøL comes back from the FIAC, I stick my gun on his head and give him some good shots. Not very constructive, but I'm mad with rage. Only my taste for profit pushes me to look for a plan B. A good beating, however justified, would cut me off from a precious distribution channel. To avoid this, I decide to play it smart. While waiting for the traitor to arrive, I drink and snort with the beautiful Pamela. Around midnight, LøL, demat, Pat, the gallery owner Laurent Strouck and a certain Christian Martin arrive. Martin was a photographer-journalist at *L'Auto-Journal* and, above all, a friend of Stéphanie Busuttil.

LøL blushes at the sight of Pam, Franck and me, seemingly calm and relaxed by the champagne. Mouths agape, the fake brothers understand that they are discovered. Their lies, cheating and betrayals are displayed before our eyes. When LøL manages to compose a fake smile of conviviality and happiness, I attack.

- Way to go, man! You're going solo. You don't even have the honesty to tell me about it, that's class. Tell me, how do you manage to sell your shit? If not, you want to send us to jail, right?

23. My clash period [End 1999]

LøL laughs *dark* yellow. He launches into an explanation as muddy as emberlificotée: basically, he is harassed by all the galleries in France; his life is excessively expensive, in spite of the tens of millions earned thanks to me; moreover, as I left for abroad, he had to replace me, he couldn't stop because I was testing the Asian market; and then, it wasn't me who was going to reproach him for having copied someone else's talent - in this case, my talent as a forger! Even if everything is not false, I interrupt his justifications with anger:

- Stop it, will you? What you've done is not right, for one thing. And, above all, your work is shit!

LøL barely paled and shrugged:

- We don't care. With Pat, everything is authenticated, so...

Pat, Strouck and Martin do not move.

- Well, LøL, I'm not going to drown the fish: we're going to change our way of working a bit. We're going to deal with the market in parallel. We're going to exchange information so we don't work on the same clients; Pat's going to get us the expertise we need; and, so the market doesn't fall apart, I'm going to teach you how to do things a little more dignified.

We agree.

This was the smartest strategy. There's no way I'm letting this guy get out of control. It's in my best interest to force him to be on top. Millions are at stake, and within reach of our bank accounts. LøL understands this, and our association is back on a sound footing. The only outstanding question is: what role does Pat play in being so close to Stéphanie Busuttil, the César workshop and Alain-Dominique Perrin? Either he is a very good friend of the widow, and she knows about the scheme; or she is foolish enough to let him fool her and make her sign his papers between two cups of tea. One thing is sure: he earns a lot of money, thanks to us but not only: in his house, a stone's throw from Matignon, at the end of an ultra-protected alley, he sells all sorts of well-known artists.

That day in 1999, we left in the early morning. We were smart to avoid making a scene. The network is reorganized. Now we have to take advantage of it. It's time for the money to come in pallets, for us and for the others: thanks to our *business*, we make the rich richer and wash the dirty money. Who would complain about that, and what about it? We are not crooks, but rich artists with great financial needs. Nothing wrong with that, as far as I know!

24. My cash period [2000]

Anxious to prevent the market from continuing to be sullied by crude forgeries, I make LøL my "pupil", as he himself will tell the cops. I take him to visit museums and galleries that exhibit New Realism and especially real works by César. I force him to buy all the catalogs of exhibitions and public sales concerning the master. I give him the contact of buyers in Saint Paul, Paris and London. I provide him with unverifiable provenances so that he can give credibility to his Caesars by claiming that they come from such and such a private collection that once existed - I am not being prejudiced, I know many!

I encourage him to take pictures of works in the galleries so that he can zoom in on the signatures. I teach him the importance of measuring sizes and paying attention to dating. I get him a special art researcher's card, which is necessary to enter the secure rooms and the reserves. I make him discover the interest of investigating, of studying all kinds of documents like the handwritten letters of the masters. I show him the different drawing techniques of César, relatively stable from the 1960s until his death.

Every day or so, we go to the Richelieu library, near his home. He takes lots of notes. I lure him into the very private reserves of the François Mitterrand library so that he can discover as many elements about Caesar as possible. This is how we find, in old exhibition catalogs, sources that I myself did not know. Such discoveries are doubly valuable: impossible to trace back to these collectors in person, and indisputable traceability in case the collector asks too many questions about the provenance before lining up his millions! You have to be sharp and anticipate the obligatory questions. In short, LøL understands that he can't be a forger by half. He understands that he must not even aim for perfection: he must achieve it.

As long as we're playing museum rats, we don't just stop at Caesar's works. We go through the cabinet of drawings and prints of the Louvre, where I have my entries thanks to a little darling art restorer. We explore the works of Miró, Klein, Chagall, Modigliani, Fernand Léger, Basquiat, Robert Combas, Arman, Warhol, multiplying notes and photos. During the *weekend*, armed with this scrupulously classified information, we go, together or each one on his own, to provide ourselves with objects that can be used for our future creations.

At the flea markets of Saint-Ouen and Clignancourt, as well as the second-hand dealers from whom, for years, Franck and I have been buying old canvas-crocks which, once scratched, stripped of their unspeakable subjects, can be used to paint Modigliani and Léger. LøL tried his hand at this until he obtained spectacular results. He will sell a Modigliani made with tar for black, a *Portrait of a woman with a long neck* dated from the beginning of the twentieth century. Profit: the equivalent of three million euros, generously provided by a Parisian senator. I also gave LøL the press in Gennevilliers where César worked, which allowed him to operate almost continuously. In the weeks that followed, at random in the Parisian galleries, I saw side by side the works of LøL's two periods, the null period and the perfect period!

At least one man was quickly delighted by our double creativity: Laurent Strouck. He knows us well, LøL and me; and the reality of our activity did not escape him... on the contrary! The man has millions to invest. So he can, in the same day, buy from LøL the equivalent of 300 000 € of works, and then come to my *flat* to raid what I have just had compressed in Grasse. As soon as I call him, he arrives with *cash* and his beautiful wife.

His dream: to have the exclusivity of the works that LøL and I create. We can always dream...

We organize private dinners in his 350 m2 avenue Georges V. I come with my *chic girl-lovers*; LøL arrives with Pamela the fabulous. During the dinner, we play with Laurent. LøL and I have brought hundreds of authenticated drawings by César. Laurent presents us with three bags full of bills and tells us to choose. One bag contains the equivalent of €100,000, the second €200,000 and the last €400,000. In exchange, no matter which bag we find, Laurent will keep everything we have brought "from Caesar". What madness! I have the impression that we are all rich as hell. Money doesn't matter anymore. What excites us is to play, not even to win or lose. The game starts when we are drunk on Chablis and other alcohols, not forgetting our dashes of powder. LøL takes a bag; I choose mine; Laurent puts his hand on the works. We decide not to open these surprise bags until late at night. LøL has only raised the equivalent of €100,000. This makes him laugh because the sum represents at least ten times the basic value of the fake real ones. I took mine - bingo, 400 000! In any case, we were three winners. That's where we were! If Caesar saw this from above, would he laugh? Maybe he would, knowing his humor...

My individual buyers carry the *cash* in grocery bags marked "Leader Price" or "Ed the Grocer". They arm themselves with Colt 357 Magnum. Delivering the bills to me at night in large quantities, they are afraid of being robbed by small street thugs. The Halles district, historically hot, is not far from my *flat* in the rue Saint-Honoré. But let's be serious: the slob bag trick is crude: my buyers

24. M CASH PERIOD [2000]

ooze left-bank *looks* from every pore of their skin. They're driving the brand new Mercedes ML 500 AMG, W163 version, nothing to do with the *cheap* stores they're supposed to have shopped in!

When I receive the bags, I deposit most of it in *offshore* accounts that accept cash; I keep some of it loose, rolled into balls in my apartment, for "overheads" - food, champagnes, vodka, nose fees, clothes, trendy restaurants, ultra-chic clubs, including huge tips to valets and security guards at clubs like vip, La Véranda at Cathy Guetta's, Queen, Man Ray, Matisse, Barfly, Nirvana and Millionaire. I go wherever I can get blown up with my bimbos and the buddies of my staff of forgers. For us, money is a sesame as much as, for others, fame. It opens the doors of these *very closed* places. *Hello, jet set!*

LøL, proud of himself and the new quality of his forgery work, sends me emails to challenge me by proving that he is on top and always supported by Pat. He tells me about his successes, the millions he earns every month by making mountains of Léger, César, Modigliani, Klein sponges; and he omits to thank me for giving him the golden key that gave him access to this so profitable Parisian art market.

He talks about the parties he organizes in Paris and London: *hype* parties, vernissages with sales of authenticated forgeries and works by young artists like Erró. Copying my strategy, he invests part of his earnings in a collection of real works, especially those of Combas or artists of the Figuration narrative. He resells, he buys, surrounds himself with big collectors who, themselves, speculate on art. He explains to me that, just like me, he is harassed by Parisian collectors - the same as me - from the left bank as well as the right bank. In the *auction houses* of London, New York and Paris, he places his Cesarean works for public sale. They send me the catalogs of these great institutions, which are also visible on the net. And what about me? Well, I am happy for him!

To tell the truth, I'm especially happy that he's flooding the market while leaving me in the shade. The more he works abroad, far from Paris, the better I feel. I am aware that there is a risk of falling; but I am certain that we will fall rich. It is obvious. We have made and sold more than two thousand authenticated works since the death of the master of compressions, making collectors and art dealers roar with joy. We are not far from having reached a form of plenitude!

25. A period too much [2000]

LøL and Martin, the guy we met after the opening of the FIAC, get along very well. They have in common their passion for Italian cars. Martin is the son-in-law of the great portraitist Francis Giacobetti, himself a good friend of César. Giacobetti was the official photographer of Shisheido cosmetics. He was a well-known owner of a 1961 Ferrari 250 California with which he crashed in Neuilly in 1985. Having heard about this accident, César proposed him to compress what was left of this Ferrari of collection - in this case the front mask with the grille, the wings and the initials of the *scuderia*. This project did not materialize. Martin, on the other hand, supplied Caesar with luxury cars, Rolls, Porsches, Ferraris and Bentleys. Caesar was a lover of women, money and rare cars!

Remembering the accident, LøL and Martin decide to take care of the Ferrari, of which only thirty examples have left the factory in Modena. This extraordinary toy, crashed and compressed fifteen years earlier, LøL cut it up with a blowtorch. He kept the front mask, the hood, the headlights tubing, and the grille with its prancing horse logo. Martin and him transport these two and a half square meters of dented red metal, through Paris, dragging this metal of a hundred kilos on the sidewalks since no cab has accepted to load this mass on its roof not to scratch its poor working tool.

At the end of their fatigue, they arrive at the parking lot of a roller rental company. They put down their burden, exhausted, covering it with a dozen blankets, protecting this nameless "thing" already shattered, as if it were Lalique crystal glassware. They choose a roll and pass it dozens of times on this "protected thing", so as to flatten it completely and to flatten the grille decorated with the prancing horse.

A few hours later, after the roller has gone every which way, they remove the protections and covers. The magic has happened. A perfectly executed, aesthetic work appears, where one recognizes the front of this Ferrari but all flat. Over the years, the red has cracked and slightly peeled off the aluminum. When I see the result, I can only be admiring.

LøL and Martin are also satisfied with the result of their tedious work. Their strength, determination and ideas have resulted in a sublime and very Caesar-like work. The spirit of the master is respected. Homage to you, Caesar!

This time, it is by truck that they transport the carcass that has become a work of art. Direction: the carpenter. The craftsman cuts a plywood background of three meters by two, fixes the hanging tubes to install in relief, on this previously bleached background, the red hood where we can clearly recognize the prancing horse. The hood, entirely flattened, is placed at fifty centimeters of the bottom and covered with Plexiglas after having been signed with the grinder: Caesar. What a masterpiece!

Stéphanie Busuttil delivers the certificate of authenticity behind the photo of the work with its description, the backdated date of manufacture, all stamped with Caesar's thumb, the stamp of the workshop as well as the history of this work dictated by Martin to Caesar's staff, so as to complete the traceability of this superb sculpture.

After consulting me, LøL decided to sell his creation in Saint-Paul through the Retelet gallery that I had indicated to him. His goal: to have Retelet present it to Michael Schumacher, who lived in the Hauts de Saint-Paul. Immediately, I explain to LøL that he has the wrong target. Knowing the driver and his entourage, I assure him that, at no price, the driver, as superstitious as he is talented, would hang a compressed Ferrari on one of his walls. He owns about thirty Formula 1 cars, all in perfect condition, kept out of sight in the basement of his megaproperty. I can't imagine him waking up before a race with this nightmarish vision!

The Retelet gallery, already feeling the big profits he will make on the back of LøL, gives him an advance equivalent to 30 000 € against the deposit of this masterpiece. Retelet is convinced that all collectors of exceptional automobiles will be big potential customers. He therefore put his new acquisition up for sale for the equivalent of €450,000.

Far from stopping there, LøL also created a splendid oil on canvas work, typical of Fernand Léger's American period and, it seems, perfectly executed, on an old painting recovered I don't know where, redone and stripped. He entrusted it to Pat so that he could sell it, which he did for the equivalent of 600 000 €. The artist was paid in record time.

Except that, patatras! A few weeks later, in New York, at Christie's, LøL realized that the painting had been sold at the hammer, to a Russian collector, for 1.5 million euros. The problem? Pat had already received a 20% commission on the €600,000 the piece was officially worth.

Less conciliatory than me, LøL, mad with rage to have been cheated, barges into his friend's house and puts a Walter PPK 9mm calibre on his head. He demands 400 000 € more. Pat, beaten to a pulp, on his stomach, signs a check to LøL who takes advantage of the situation to empty his two magazines into the glass roof of

25. A period too much [2000]

the home studio, breaking everything and shooting the works of art that Pat had on deposit and that belonged to collectors wishing to dispose of their heritage. Pat did not press charges. For a few weeks, he was hospitalized with multiple fractures and a smashed mouth. Pat, the thief, is in pieces!

LøL comes to me, furious. I cut it short. I leave Jean Roch's. I was at the VIP, on the Champs-Élysées. I come back with three of my favorite bimbos. I am not in the same trip as my "student". It's seven o'clock in the morning, I'm full of bubbles and snow, and all I can think about is the upcoming sex session. He, on the other hand, is in his delirium. He wants me to help him burn down Pat's house while our ex-partner is moaning in the hospital. I send him packing. This guy is going crazy. Too much *coke*, too much money, too much arrogance. He's going off the deep end, I couldn't do anything for him. He needs to calm down first, but I'm ashamed of his behavior. Christine and I have introduced him to a world of *hype*, class and glamour; he is proving unable to hold back his animal instincts, intolerant of frustration. I'm not a moralist, I get angry sometimes, but I find it distressing to persist in my hatred. Hasn't he taken enough revenge? For God's sake, we're not those little robbers who kill for nothing, nor are we those mad dogs who tear each other apart! I decide to get away from this lunatic, never to see him again... and to enjoy my bimbos, no way!

26. My Flemish period [2001]

After Pat's beating, I want a change of scene. I contact the gallery of Guy Pieters to whom my ex-companions have sold an astronomical quantity of fake Caesars made by Franck and me. The guy has unlimited resources. He has six galleries, in Europe and in Los Angeles.

In Antwerp, he reigns over 2000 m² of modern art, *pop art* and New Realism. This unique reserve of the greatest works of art available on the market is a heavenly place. I love to stroll around and visit the armored vaults of its storage.

A branch of the company is located a few kilometers from the Modern Art Foundation, in Latem, on the edge of the lake, in the center of a village inhabited by the new fortunes of Flanders. Here, life seems lascivious, passive, protected, like Barbie and Ken's village. Surreal! This gallery is managed by Guy Priels, who will become our privileged interlocutor for our future transactions with Pieters.

A third gallery is located in Knokke, close to the Flemish casino paradise, with billionaires whose fortunes were made through diamonds, new technologies and money laundering *via* casinos, in addition to the old institutionalized fortunes.

Guy Pieters had started his career by opening this gallery in Knokke; five years later, he would have been incarcerated in Belgium for having concealed a fake Magritte. This did not prevent him from creating a more important gallery, that of Latem, where he exhibited and sold Yves Klein, Arman, Nicky de Saint Phalle, whom he was able to approach thanks to his relations in financial circles, to Roger Niellens, the director of the Knokke casino, to Jef Van Turnhout, and to Mr. Peulof.

The money helps finance the purchase of artworks and the opening of other contemporary art galleries. Works were purchased in large quantities. Among them, countless Caesars were sold to wealthy Flemish industrialists who did not hesitate to pay several million euros for a work that was only worth a tenth. With the fortune he amassed, Guy Pieters opened a fourth gallery in Saint-Paul, paid the equivalent of 1.5 million euros; and he bought himself a superb villa worth 4.5 million euros, two hundred meters from the Maeght Foundation. The gallery is located in the golden triangle of art. It still sells *pop art*, Warhol, Robert Indiana, Arman, César, new realists, Sam Francis, etc.

The appointment is made for a Saturday afternoon. In my Mercedes-Benz SL 55 AMG convertible, I take a jumble of works, including lithos by Picasso and Miró, as well as two unauthenticated César prints. When I arrived, I noticed that his gallery contained monumental works by Bernard Venet, many by Klein, Alechinsky, Warhol, Folon... There were a number of César's that I recognized as being my own work and that had been sold to them by Pat and LøL. All were certified. I soon realized that all the prints and drawings sold in France came through Antwerp.

Among my proposals, he stops on the cuts.

- How many do you want? he asks me.

- The equivalent of 100,000 euros each.

- Do you have certificates?

- Uh... no, why?" I answer, playing the foolish heir. I don't know any experts. Besides, I've had these works for about twenty years.

I got them from Jan Kjerulff, the son-in-law of Helmut Kaiser Kraft, the industrialist!

The only name of my late friend Jan seems to reassure the gallery owner. He offers me a check. I refuse. I want *cash*, so I argue:

- At this time, no bank is open anymore, and I can't wait until Monday for it to reopen: I'm leaving tonight for Denmark!

The Fleming calls his secretary. He wants to negotiate the two cuts for the equivalent of €150,000. I argue a little, looking upset. I give in for €160,000 and sign a receipt when, surprise, he asks me:

- What currency do you want to be paid in? Dollars? Swiss Francs? French Francs ?

I ask for French francs. A moment later, the secretary brings the sum in new bills. The gallery owner removes the two compressions and tells me that he is a buyer of *pop art* and New Realism. Then he returned to the back of his gallery. Shortly after, I learned that he was in mourning: he had bought a Ferrari for his only son who had been killed the day before.

We stay and party in Antwerp before starting weekly trips between Paris and Grasse to feed the Flemish trade. By working directly with Guy Pieters, I no longer need to go through Pat to authenticate the works. Le Flamand was close to the master, he is a friend of Stéphanie Busuttil and Denyse Durand-Ruel who, since 1964, have been in charge of archiving the anarchic work of César. I sell my creations without a certificate or intermediary. I make hundreds of drawings, at a rate of about ten a day, always studies of chickens and centaurs. I invent formats that are much larger than those of César, who did not exceed 20x30cm; mine reach 100x80cm and are much more coveted!

Strange as it may seem, all of them are sold on a daily basis, for the equivalent of 6000 € per drawing given in cash. Most of my production goes to Pieters, but I reserve some pieces for Laurent Strouck. I constantly have new orders. I have to invent new hens, including hens in rollerblades and fishnet stockings, even *drag-queen* hens with Caesar's head. I adorn some of them with feathers from my pillows. Just like that, to be delirious. However, Caesar, in spite of his humor, would never have done that!

I collect old license plates, old rusty jerry cans that have contained gasoline, old Honda P50 motorcycles with the engine on the rear wheel, as well as cars from which we remove the interiors, tires, engine, windows, so as to keep only the carcasses that we compress in Grasse. The results, the choice of objects are Caesar-like. All that remains is to sign them and send them by Air France Cargo, direction rue Saint-Honoré, in Paris. The works of art are only held for a few hours before being sent directly to Belgium.

Having understood my trick and the process, the workers of the junkyard manufacture directly for me. When I arrive, the cuts are finished. I pay them the best ones. They make them again and again. They reserve the aluminum juice cans, the Coca-Cola cans and the beers for me; and they even end up having fun creating compressions while I'm going back and forth between Paris and Grasse. It's up to me to age the result. At no time does a very sharp collector, ultra connoisseur and made suspicious because of the considerable number of sculptures on the international market, certified, of course, by Stéphanie Busuttil's staff and by the Fleming, detect the slightest error.

When I arrive in the scrapyard, the workers of art, pressers and compressors, clean the metal waste remaining in "the press"; then they remove grease and impurities. I can then organize the layout of the objects that I place with meticulousness while the crushes are of several tons. Chance does the rest. The workers are bluffed, happy to see this cube, a perfect prism that will have to be refined again and again to bring it closer to the truth of the master.

I leave my assistants huge tips. I often give them the uncrushed toys for their children or other items for their families; and when they have the funny idea of asking me indiscreet questions, I always give the same answer: I am an interior decorator!

Some days, in the middle of trucks full of scrap metal to be compressed, I arrive in a Mercedes with a trunk full of toys to destroy. The toy cars fit together and come out intertwined. I have never seen such perfect and balanced sculptures on the market; I have always wondered if Caesar could have made this kind of compression. That day, I extracted three parallelepipeds of 50x50x50cm and one of 50x50x20cm. They don't need any retouching, except for the signature. They stagnate in my apartment because I don't want to sell them as usual. I like them. These works, I thought and realized them. I had fun refining them. Above all, I respected the spirit of Caesar. I know that the goal is to disperse them on the market. In general, the day after their completion, they are packed and delivered by UPS directly to my home-workshop-gallery.

I sell each of the most important compressions, beautiful, colorful and playful little toy cars in 1/18th that I buy new by pallets. I want yellow, red, black, and only small Ferrari. When I deliver my creation, I demand the equivalent of 100 000 €. The Fleming does not discuss the price anymore. He suspects that I will come back to supply him exclusively. He pays me *cash* and takes everything. He even travels to Paris to negotiate other deals that he pays, as usual, in cash and without invoice.

For my personal collection, I hide the most beautiful of my creations. It is also the smallest and the finest. I have it installed on a black Plexiglas base. The largest, heaviest, most imposing ones sell better. I often have the impression that Caesar's work is sold less by its beauty than by weight and cubic meter.

As soon as I deliver, other gallery owners, auctioneers, auction houses like Sotheby's or Christie's, and all the little fish in between, go hunting for wealthy buyers. Speculators buy and resell works of art on the same day without really checking anything about their authenticity, their provenance, their history - never mind the important traceability that exists between the artist and the real collector.

The only way not to die is to be heard, to go down in history by leaving the imprint of an idea. An outstanding artist never ages. He is always alive through his work. Counterfeiters make him prolific and perpetuate a work that nobody really knows. That's what keeps me going: I want to understand the artist's discourse, to continue to invent works that he didn't make but that he could have created. This should always be done by an enlightened art lover, an expert worthy of the name, and not a rightful claimant who signs for a fee everything that is submitted to him, even what he knows was never done by the artist he is closest to. This is what is scandalous and what puts off a young painter. This is what is immoral, not the creation of forgeries. The real forgers are passionate. They visit galleries. They rub shoulders with uncorrupted professionals in order to improve themselves.

I once knocked on the door of a real expert for a pen and ink sketch by Marcel Gromaire. The expert charged me a few hundred euros before telling me that the work was fake for reasons I prefer to forget. In spite of him, I contacted the Galerie de la Présidence, rue du Faubourg-Saint-Honoré. During a vernissage, I met a direct descendant of the artist. After having given me an appointment at his home, he told me that it was indeed a work of Marcel and that the little child in the scene of the drawing was himself. I left with my certificate of authenticity and the fascinating history of this work. I still have it in my collection. It only cost me the pleasure of hearing the sound of truth, and of seeing the emotion of Gromaire's descendant with whom I spent two or three hours looking through books, admiring drawings, inks, oils on canvas to learn about this artist.

27. My messed up period [2001]

One day, knowing that I was still making huge profits, LøL barges into my *flat-gallery* without warning. Clueless, lost, empty and tired of having done too many Caesars. The fortune he has just amassed? Blown up. So who knows if the source stamped "Éric Piedoie Le Tiec" could not provide him with new ideas, new concepts, or even give him the contact information of his clients?

Desperate, LøL comes up with the absurd idea, not devoid of humor but incompatible with the spirit of César, of buying new objects like flags, children's trains, rails, wagons, in short anything and everything, then buying Araldite glues, wooden panel backgrounds cut to the right sizes and white paint to cover them with a brush. Then, we would create the Plexiglas boxes, sign Caesar at the bottom with pencil, and sell the whole thing to galleries and collectors, in kit form, to be assembled by oneself. LøL is delirious but serious! Convinced that, if César had heard this idea, he would have had my ex-partner compressed, I decline the offer. Vexed, LøL left.

Nothing to confuse me. With Franck, we decide to tackle new types of works, on the model of what Caesar made at the end of his life. Indeed, until his death, he surrounded himself with a staff executing his concepts. All that remains is to list the works that we never made.

After that, we make *compression portraits*. For this, we cut out panels of wood-lattice of 90x110 cm in general, but also other formats. Franck whitens the panels with matte paint in order to build the background. On the three quarters of this bleached and quickly dried background, I draw, with graphite, a cube in perspective.

I bought three hundred boxes of pipe matches and wood glue - a glue that becomes transparent as it dries. Once the cube is drawn, coated with this magic glue, I throw all the matches inside my perspective, several centimeters thick, in a spontaneous way, as one throws the Mikado. The matches overflow, so they sometimes erase the lines in graphite. I want at least five centimeters thick. I rob the tobacco shops in the area to buy all their boxes. The tobacconists must wonder what I am up to!

For lack of setting fire to Paris, I create cubes that are so many trompe-l'oeil portraits of a compression. The loose matches are arranged in perspective, the red tips illuminating the composition. Everything is perfect, everything fits together. I airbrush one side of the cube to reveal the light and shadow side of the *match compression portrait*. This gives it a foundation. The perspective takes on volume. All I have to do now is to grey out the base of this sculpture with pencil, with large cross strokes, to give it a virtual base. I fix the thousands of lines of graphite with hair spray, and I affix the signature at the bottom right: César, 1987. The finished work, I put it under a Plexiglas case and I move on.

I give our new creations to the Fleming, who is himself a great connoisseur of Caesar's work. In *cash*, without an invoice, he paid me the equivalent of 300,000 € before obtaining the certificates, so certain was he of obtaining authentication. Later, as I walked around, I found some of them on the walls of certain galleries in the Carré rive gauche, on the Avenue Matignon and in the auction catalogs of the greatest auctioneers in Paris!

Continuing my diversification, I buy five hundred copies of small flags of about fifteen countries that can be found in the shopkeepers, in front of the Louvre. In the same way as for the compression portraits, I repeat the same composition with the flags. Crumpled, glued, superimposed, they form a similar portrait. I have reduced the size to make a series of about fifteen different countries. Thus, they can be hung next to each other, 50x80 cm, mounted under Plexiglas. I have a homogeneous collection of fifteen countries. I sell all of them... except for Italy, Brazil, Japan and Jamaica, whose boxes I have lined up horizontally, on a wall in my *flat-atelier*.

Not surprisingly, the compressed flags of the eleven countries are duly authenticated. Armed with photos of my creations, Guy Pieters obtains his archive numbers and the certificates of the Caesar staff, which he sticks on the back of the panels. These works are sold to a collector who buys the eleven boxes for the equivalent of 750 000 €. The profits are considerable for the Fleming, who has the correction to thank us warmly. I know who his buyers are, but I say nothing, preferring to create in the shadows. I also know that these works will be put up for sale all over Europe, in Antwerp and in the big fairs like the FIAC. I am amused to see them reproduced, listed, numbered, at prohibitive prices, in the catalogs of these *auction houses* and on the Internet!

We produce, on panel, enamel coffee pot compressions of all colors. We produce hundreds of these new "Tributes to Morandi" signed by César. On *weekends*, in Saint-Cloud, Franck buys an industrial quantity of old coffee pots at the flea market. This way, we are sure to be constantly supplied. I even reserve the sizes of the coffee pots and their colors, imagining the mixtures of enamel powders and future compositions, forming what César called the great parade of coffee pots, frozen in their momentum for eternity.

Franck perfectly adapts the mixtures of colors, sometimes leaving, between two coffee pots, the imprint of a missing coffee pot, as if it had escaped from the pack. Disappeared, misplaced: only the enamel deters it. The new tributes to Morandi are composed of two to ten coffee pots in a row, depending on the desired format.

Franck produces four to five of them per week, perfectly executed, ready to be transported to the Fleming when they are not dispatched all over the *arty* planet. The Cesaresque coffee pots and their transactions are as tight as the coffee they contained! We sell them in batches of six to ten at a time, every two weeks, primarily at the Pieters gallery, with prices ranging from €30,000 to €100,000, depending on the format. Always the same scenario: preparation, composition, final assembly and sale without expertise. The Fleming takes care of the authentication.

For the remaining pieces, I don't need a certificate. I sell them directly to the same galleries in Europe, the United States and Korea. No less than two hundred "Tributes to Morandi" have been produced by Franck's studio thanks to the complicity of the art world and the artist's entourage. We also make compressions of packets of Gauloises, Marlboros, champagne corks, as well as portraits of condom compressions that I order from my pharmacist, who delivers them to me in packages of two thousand. Thus, we realize the compressions of unrolled condoms, unwrapped and, especially, dried of the gel with which they are coated. Otherwise, impossible to stick them on panel.

The floor of the studio and the apartment is covered with condoms of all colors, drying in the sun. Franck makes about thirty compressions that I finish by greying them with graphite and signing them. With a few exceptions, all of them are sold at Le Flamand. As for the carpet of condoms, it could have stayed on the floor as a decoration, it was surreal and avant-garde. *Safe floor*, very protected!

Despite our disagreement, LøL is still harassing me. I feel that he wants to plagiarize my work again, to steal the ingredients, the manufacturing information and especially the signatures. He wants to know who my various buyers are in Japan, Italy, Belgium, Europe and the United States, no less.

He continues to make many works, even if his interpretations are not always in the spirit of the master. I go to his house less and less, only to find out that we produce too much work... and that he and Pamela have crazy needs. That explains why LøL has to produce and sell all the time. This couple is well matched in terms of *love-sex-trash*, but the lifestyle they lead puts us all in danger. Our works are exchanged on the international markets in an industrial way and risk to confuse us and to lead us straight to jail. I see them everywhere: his, mine, Frank's, in Europe and on the walls of collectors!

LøL has blown through cubic meters of cash in a short period of time without giving anything back to anyone. I could follow my animal instinct in front of all the times he turned his coat. I have an itch, but my reason tells me that revenge is a forest where I risk getting lost. Better to watch him from afar, let him act and note for the record the times he crosses the white lines of respect, friendship and the rest. So often, because the bugger has some, messed up plans! An example? With his friend Christian Martin, LøL offers to sell me large blank sheets of paper, already signed César, with the thumbprint on the signature. I refuse his offers; I know where this print comes from! I don't need anyone to validate the work that my brother and I were doing. Certainly not from him.

I see them again, him and the other parasite, at the party given by Pamela and LøL. *Dress code* ? Chickens and centaurs, of course! Welcome to the feathered centaurs, boa around the neck! My bimbos, in gallinaceous perched on Dior stilts, fishnet stockings and Venetian masks representing hens with red and green crests, transparent bustiers, arms covered with feathers mounted on fluorescent green latex gloves covering the whole of their arms up to their shoulders, pink, red, multicolored ostrich feathers, fixed in the lacing of the bustiers by the back made by John Galliano. Caesar's sketches gave life to all this human fauna, successful delusions from the work of the master. I see in a corner Martin, that evening, without *dress code*! Between two *sex-love* deliriums on David Guetta, *coke* and champagne lighting up this chic *event* "tribute to Caesar", I retire to snort with my three gallinaceous bimbos who are stripped in the soft hell of flying feathers.

A big surprise, I see hundreds of drawings, always the same subjects, signed, finished or being finished, more or less finished. I take LøL to task and ask him, in *a soft way*, not to put his failed works on the market. Now very active again, he starts to make fake Caesars again! Financial worries oblige! He tells me that all the works I have seen have their certificates, except those in progress. I understand that these certificates do not come from Pat but from Martin.

LøL is at the end of the road. He dishonors the master of New Realism. I have a hunch that LøL will stop creating Caesars. He must have found other sources of enrichment. I don't care! I powder my nose and run away from LøL to find myself in a huge henhouse where chickens and plucked centaurs are intermingling. My bimbos being already in action, I find others to play at sex. The sound of "Guetta", perfect, resounds until Karl Lagerfeld's studio who, not far from there, phones to come and have fun with us. Welcome, Karl!

28. My panic period [June 2001]

With my friend Anissa, I walk past the Anne Lettrée gallery. In the window, I discover a considerable number of compressions, drawings and portraits signed by César, which LøL and Pat had made several months earlier. Since I don't know the gallery owner, we enter and visit the exhibition, asking for details about prices, periods and rarity of the pieces. I learn more than I expected. None of the pieces I made are in this gallery. I immediately recognized the crude work of centaur and chicken drawings, 1/18 scale compressions of small cars in Plexiglas, ugly portraits of Marlboro packets compressions, as well as all sorts of fake sculptures that, Anne Lettrée tells me, "come from friends." In reality, they are remnants of LøL's first period, co-created with Pat before their separation. They remain unsold... and for good reason: the prices are astronomical. They go from the equivalent of 10 000 € for a small drawing, not finished, just scribbled, to the equivalent of 100 000 € for the compressions. I leave happy to have not seen any of my work in the middle of these infamous works. Anissa and I run to Le Flore to get drunk and laugh at such obvious deceptions.

The Lettrée affair did not end there. Learning that I have known Arman for a long time, the gallery owner asked me if I could provide her with some sculptures. She too is a good friend of the artist. She wanted to organize a retrospective of the artist, but when she contacted him in New York, he told her that he had no stock of sculptures to lend. I immediately thought that since she only exhibits fake Caesars, stamped LøL and Pat, Arman must have realized that this place could be detrimental to him.

For some reason, I agree to do this gallery owner a favor. I contacted a friend, Sidi, who confirmed that he knew where to find two to three hundred works by the master Arman. I am astonished. He provides me with professional quality photos of all these works that are in his residence-workshop in Vence, ready to be sent to Asia for a big retrospective. When I present the photos to the gallery, Anne Lettrée is shocked. She became furious: according to her, it was impossible to gather so many pieces of Arman's work since even she had not succeeded. She accuses me of deceiving her about the provenance of the works. Embarrassed, I asked Sidi to confirm the authenticity of the works. It was a waste of time, the dealer did not believe a word of it.

There is reason to be offended, indeed! All the eras of the master's work are brought together. Still furious, the lady tried to contact Arman. He is unreachable, whether in Paris, New York or Vence. She gave me back the photos, telling me that there was a wolf. Without saying a word, I think: "With the pack of wolves in your gallery, there's no reason to be offended, my dear! I hand over the professional prints to Sidi, who can't believe it. I am afraid that, because of this affair, the gallery owner will alert her husband, a cop, which would risk harming my business, in these troubled times.

Immediately, I contacted my entourage, in particular Christian Martin, who was still in Paris, to whom I showed these photos. I learned that he was also a relation of Arman's and that he had taken all the photos of the works himself, before the master prepared them, had them packed and insured for transport to Asia.

The photos were to be used for the catalog raisonné of the upcoming exhibition. The art world is tiny!

Not put off by this absurd episode, Sidi introduced me to the president of the Arab Chamber of Commerce, rue de Presbourg, in the eighth arrondissement of Paris. He wanted to show me a number of works that Saudi collectors wanted to sell. On the spot, I was introduced to Lofti Velhassimii, the former owner of Air Liberté and part of Fouquet's, a great art lover. He wishes to bail out by selling impressionist and modern works.

Amongst the Matisse, Monet and Picasso hanging everywhere, what a surprise to see fifty or so Caesars on sale! These mediocre fakes are all by LøL. I am seized by an irrepressible, compulsive and dismaying urge to laugh. Once the crisis was over, I declined the offer to buy the Caesars *made by* LøL and Pat. I buy four gouache drawings by Picasso, listed, with their history and above all their certificate of authenticity, for the equivalent of 150 000 €. I place a transfer order directly by telephone, from my company account in Brussels to the *offshore* account of the famous penniless seller. After having left his 10% commission to Sidi, I tell him about the Caesars he is trying to sell. In reality, I understand that he knew about it and wanted to cheat me. He was waiting for me to test the quality of the Caesars, to know if he could sell them elsewhere. The human race inspires me only disgust, when a betrayal deviates from friendship. I forget about this guy for good. Well, almost: I will see him again later in police custody, where he remained free and uncharged.

In spite of the troubled feeling that we are running to our loss, I continue to work with Franck, my magician brother. In the secure setting of his studio, safe from the possible eyes of the cops, he makes portraits of stamp compressions that I buy in packages of twenty thousand, in bulk, on Rue Drouot. The finished works, we bring them directly to Flanders, to the gallery of one of the artistic directors of Latem's gallery, Guy Priels. We leave to deliver them with my rocket, at 300 km/h, or by night train. We slaughter our last cards...

On Pat's order, Franck is working on four series of coffee pots crushed and mounted on panels. Once the work is finished, I realize that, by helping my brother, I am putting the pressure of Pat on him. Nevertheless, we make these four pieces in a very short period of time. Three are mountable and negotiated the equivalent of 55 000 € each. The fourth one, it's me who missed it. I mixed an epoxy glue incorrectly and the coffee pots in the fourth piece slipped to the bottom of the frame. Glue drips messed up the piece, making it unsellable for my taste. This screw-up increases the risk of being spotted. Nevertheless, Pat insists on seeing the unglued piece. It has to be completely redone. He nevertheless takes it, promising to have it restored by one of his magicians from the Louvre. Indeed, one month later, my infamous mistake has taken on a Caesar-like appearance; and the piece is paid for like the others. We receive the equivalent of 250 000 €.

This time, I decided to stop working with this mafia of madmen and unscrupulous dealers. I turn directly to the big auction houses in Northern Europe, London and the United States. Pat pesters me on the phone. He has the feeling that the Piedoie Le Tiec gold mine is slipping away from him. As I remained firm in my position, he started blackmailing me and threatening me: if I stopped working with him and he had problems, he would turn against me and throw everything away. I remind him that I know about his relationship with Caesar's heir and the Cartier Foundation. In other words, he shouldn't play this game with me: he would fall, and his friends with him. I never saw or heard him whine again, but my hunch was confirmed: this was a time of panic!

29. My *crash test* period [July 2001]

In July 2001, Christian Martin told me that, since the beginning of the César affair, he had used his connections to help LøL obtain its certificates. LøL never had any financial recognition for him. So he offered to sell me the thumb stamp of César for the equivalent of 5000 €. He also has the stamp of the École nationale des beaux-arts de Paris that César, and later Stéphanie Busuttil, used to affix to the back of the photos of the works that LøL and I were making. Of course, I refused this offer, but since I felt sorry for him, I offered to help me set up an exhibition in the United States. He immediately accepted. He knows that I am a straight shooter. There is no risk that I will blur it.

We are short on materials to prepare for the American show. In my collection, I have some real Caesars of indisputable provenance, including a child's pedal car, a small Ferrari from the 1950s that had belonged to Richard Fulton as a child. Richard had asked Caesar to compress the child's car on my advice, in order to sell it to pay for his vices. I was present when the toy was crushed, and I bought back the compression, with a picture of Caesar holding it in his arms, looking satisfied with his work.

When Martin sees this intimate room in my apartment, he suggests that I go and buy about twenty small cars at the flea market and at various second-hand shops. I accept. We decide to fill a Espace Renault with these rusty but soulful toys. At the Samaritaine, we buy about a hundred toys similar to those I had already worked on: 1/18 scale cars, old Ferraris, Mercedes and Cadillacs, about a hundred. We empty the shelves and bring all these toys to Grasse.

I go down to the Colombe d'Or with Martin. The next day, I visit Guy Pieters, exposing him our idea of exhibition in Miami with the manufacture of works to support it. The Fleming proposes to sell him the totality of the collection whereas we did not even make it. He wants to exhibit it at Art Paris, at the Carrousel du Louvre. I gave in partially, and signed a partnership agreement for half of the works.

We go to the Maiarelli junkyard, in Plan-de-Grasse, where I have my little habits. We spend the day compressing cars with pedals. The result is as good as I expected. All we have to do is to touch up the parts with a hammer, at the corners. Martin takes care of this simple operation. The rest is dismantled and torched, as if we were doing mini *crash tests*.

We left after having offered once again small cars to the workers for their children. Martin's Renault Espace goes back to Paris. I stay a few more days at the Colombe d'Or with a Swedish friend, rubbing shoulders with Bono, Rod Stewart and star artists, and enjoying the magic of the place, the climate and the festive atmosphere of the Coast in the heart of summer.

30. My car period [September 11, 2001]

My accomplice Yaël Marciano meets me in Grasse at the beginning of September. He brings works by César and Warhol for us to sell to Guy Pieters. He comes especially so that we can help the Fleming to organize the *pop art* vernissage of Robert Indiana. All the works arrived by freight in Nice, from Boston, and the exhibition is planned in the gallery of Saint-Paul de Vence.

We have to arrange the huge "Love" whose red and yellow electric bulbs are flashing. We spread out the sculptures in the gardens and inside the gallery, where the paintings are concentrated. I bounce some ideas off Guy, who is completely depressed because Indiana can't fly out of the U.S. due to the terrorist attacks. Our idea of bringing him in on a friend's *jet* was not successful: the American authorities blocked all takeoffs, private and commercial. This exhibition cost him more than a million dollars in freight, insurance, cranes, trucks, etc. As eight out of ten collectors are Americans, he is afraid of a flop. I reassure him as best I can by saying:

- It's going to be a hit! You exhibit the sculptures of an American artist, you have huge prisms of LOVE, what could be better than exhibiting love? In times of terrorism, it's great!

Indeed, on the evening of the opening, 60% of the exhibition is sold. I had all my relations come so that this opening would be *cool* and that, for a few hours, we would no longer think about the Twin Towers tragedy. The space is packed. I film the room. The magic of the works, the aura of the guests and the bubbles of champagne allow me to begin to realize a dream: to interview artists and collectors, moreover in uninhibited mode.

The vernissage finished, we go to dinner in Cannes. Guy and I reserved a huge table for my lawyer, my friends, as well as the VIP collectors and the Fleming's relatives. As the night progressed, we left for another evening at the Palm Beach in Cannes, until daybreak. The gendarmes will tell me later that they tried to follow us in vain. The unmarked cars were too slow, and we... we were very loaded!

Back in Paris, the compressed and retouched pedal cars are delivered by Martin, as well as the burned and damaged toys, ready to be glued on 30x60 cm panels. Between my personal works and these, it becomes almost impossible to move around my apartment. Once again, from the hell of the junkyard, we have drawn magnificent Caesars. All that remains is to sign them, which I do with my dental wheel. Martin takes care of taking pictures of the compressed pieces to get the certificates of authenticity and to illustrate the book of the exhibition we are preparing for Miami. As promised, we sell about 15 pieces to the Pieters Gallery in St. Paul for their Art Paris exhibition at the end of the month. Guy is in charge of obtaining the certificates of authenticity.

Having had a pedal car as a child, I remember the feeling of pedaling like a blur, trying to control my driving. I was four or five years old, and I had unknowingly entered the consumer society of art. Driving was insidiously preparing me to become Caesar's forger. Even today, life was tender. I was simply too lazy to pedal. I preferred to find good souls to push me. It was me, the assisted!

My imagination worked when I looked at these toys recycled into works of art. I was always the one who just wanted to have fun, laugh, be happy and communicate that joy to others.

I sell the twenty compressed pedal cars in Grasse. The Fleming wants to exhibit them in several international fairs. I know the price due to the rarity of these works; we find a compromise: the total sum approaches the equivalent of 600 000 €. He pays me half in cash, without an invoice, and promises me the rest within two months, after the exhibitions, without guessing that I won't have time to cash the balance, the drama already covering us with its shadow.

Martin surprises me by bringing me one hundred and fifty small 1/18 scale cars that he has stored in his garage. They were made during César's lifetime, in the workshop; it was Martin who gave César the idea for this type of work. Towards the end of his life, Caesar had some made by workers. We don't know how many were put on the market. Nobody knows! Each car and its respective pieces after crushing was stored in separate bags. These shattered cars became works of art to be rebuilt! Martin, attracted by the profit and the ease of execution, proposed to me to make them like the others. Why deprive yourself? The Fleming buys back all of Caesar's work, we must take advantage of it! Again, a long and meticulous work of model maker awaits me to obtain a perfect result, balanced after drying and setting under Plexiglas. To make matters worse, Franck is not in Paris to help me. Alone and drunk, I don't have the energy to start working again on the models on the carpet. But Guy Pieters is interested in thirty copies, and the gallery owners in Antwerp and Saint-Paul also want them, on condition that I produce them as soon as possible, as their exhibition dates are approaching.

At the same time, our exhibition in Miami is taking shape. Martin and I have a lot of supplies. Not wanting to make these cuts myself, I call on an unemployed neighbor. Hung, of Vietnamese origin, with whom I have an excellent relationship, is an art lover. He does not miss any of the endless parties I organize. Delicate, meticulous and composed, he is the ideal man to take care of the assembly of small cars. I give him as models the ones I have had passed on to Tajan and Cornette de Saint-Cyr and which are reproduced in their sales catalog.

I give him one hundred and fifty bags, each containing a shattered car, to be reconstructed in such a way that the effect suggests an accidental *crash*.

I provide him with the panels cut to the right size, the wall attachments to be fixed to the back of each work, what to glue, paint the backgrounds in white ... and a sum of twenty thousand francs for this work to be executed quickly.

Hung takes great pleasure in making the one hundred and fifty works. The result is perfect. Like a child, he regularly shows me the work he is working on to see what I think of it, and I always think well of him: he works without a trace of glue with a precision, cleanliness and respect that are not to be underestimated.

Of course, I didn't tell him everything about the purpose of the works, once they were finished, sticking to a vague :

- It is for an exhibition in Miami, in memory of Caesar...

Anyway, he doesn't care. He is passionate, he has fun, and he makes beautiful compositions. What he makes is simply the most beautiful work of this type, of a quality I have ever seen. With this same talent, he creates 150 pieces in about three weeks. First, he methodically installs them on the floor of his loft; then, when they are finished, he hangs them on the wall to admire and enjoy.

As for the ones I have on the walls, I would never have sold them. They come directly from César. I have six of them, arranged according to the colors and models.

While waiting for the certificates and the end of Hung's work, I sell a few works from my collection: a Basquiat, some Combas, a Miguel Barcelo. My goal: one, to finance my film projects on artists, with a crazy idea of making CD-ROMs (that was the time...) for the National Education; two, to maintain my nightlife; three, to buy young unknown contemporary artists, pieces by Cindy Sherman, English artists from Saatchi in London, from the White Cube gallery, and to get new works by the Chapman brothers. Art never stops!

31. The last meal
[September 26, 2001]

With the influx of new, authenticated works by Caesar, the market is becoming more and more volatile. The international value of the greatest French sculptor of the 20th century is stabilizing. It must be said that, in my opinion, we have produced more works than César himself! These pieces have enriched hundreds of gallery owners and collectors, and also the whole of his work: the catalogs raisonnés of the master's work are much thicker...

Every other night, we go out to party in Paris, from cabarets to hot spots, to the usual places where we meet our friends musicians, artists and models. To us, the world of the night! The beautiful starry sky! And please, until the morning! Action! *Full of* techno, vodka, well-being, that's what we are! The *top women*, the muses, the unavoidable party people, we meet them on the spot. We change places, go from *after party* to *after party*, to prolong the night until the end of the pleasures. Impossible to imagine that we are photographed and filmed at the point of hour by unfortunate *paparazzi* because of an investigation on our lives and the train which goes with it. *In retrospect,* I imagine the hours of waiting for these gendarmes-directors, pacing back and forth without managing to penetrate the holy of holies, these *flats* where we used to end our nights in delirium. I imagine them, bursting with rage, stuck in their rotten cars, having only the screen of their watch to realize the time which passes.

At the beginning of September 2001, I leave Guy Pieters a large part of the 150 works that Hung made a few weeks earlier for the equivalent of $550,000. He still owes me $200,000 from a previous sale but promises to pay me very soon. He seems appeased. Armed with the astronomical amount of Caesars we provided him, the gallery owner has enough to deal with the many contemporary art fairs that are coming up, as well as his clients in a hurry to invest or launder their fortunes.

On September 26, 2001, I organized a dinner with a dozen friends. We were celebrating with collectors, gallery owners, my friend Dominique Van Eyck, art broker, my friend-lover Anissa Benazza and our usual bimboosted love dolls of Paris fashion and endless nights.

Dominique is a sort of ant of the art market. He is constantly pestering me to provide him with works, especially large format drawings of authenticated centaurs and chickens. My confidence in his skills is limited because his buyers are as poor as he is. He spends most of his time gravitating around the Hôtel Drouot, among the second-hand dealers and small auctioneers, hoping for the good deal that never comes. Knowing the precariousness of his situation, I sometimes helped him to work. For example, one day, I made six true-false drawings accompanied by their certificate, and provided them to him, at the derisory price, a Van Eyck special, of the equivalent of ten thousand euros. In a few hours, if he's not too stupid, he can sell them for at least twice as much.

I do this in spite of myself, in spite of my convictions, reluctantly. I motivate myself by telling myself that this will help him to resurface, maybe even open up prospects for him to become a real art dealer. I want him to set himself up with a little more money than he was making through his selflessness and honesty. Of course, he is not in the confidence of my activity of manufacture of false Caesars; but, as long as he has real certificates, I am quiet and I have good conscience. He pays me the next day, at the scheduled time, and asks me if I still have merchandise to provide him. I gave in twice more.

When dinner is over, I stay with Anissa. We are tired from partying for days. Our friends leave around four in the morning, which is unusual in our circle. Anissa has no obligations for the next day, and I rarely have any: it's time to cuddle!

32. My period *under arrest* [September 27, 2001]

At six o'clock, the legal time for the arrests, we hear knocks and verbal summonses to open the door of my apartment.

Anissa runs to close the last locks on the front door. I learned that the gendarmes were suspicious of our presence, knowing that we went out every night. They call my cell phone, hoping to hear it ring - which might indicate my presence - or thinking that I would answer; but they go straight to my voice mail. I take advantage of the last few moments to deal with the most pressing problems. I destroy all the data on my computer, empty the photos and dismantle the hard disk that I destroy in the bathroom; *a priori, there is* nothing left to find in the PC. I also burn the diskettes of photos, the digital cassettes proving the fabrications, containing the images of openings, of gallery owners, of people I don't want to see involved in what awaits me.

I also take all the photo prints, about a hundred of them, as well as bills and documents from foreign banks. I put everything in the hot tub and set it on fire until it burned to the ground, leaving any further evidence of my activities. It is hell. The flames rise to the ceiling and lick the walls. The smoke is unbreathable. The bay window, open to the maximum, lets out a black smoke.

The smell of burning chemicals forced us to protect ourselves with masks and wet scarves. Dantesque, the atmosphere! I cause drafts to dissipate the black smoke of evidence of crime, and the white smoke of an impending arrest. The *flat overlooks* two inner courtyards, and they entered through the wrong one. I take the opportunity to destroy the dangerous DV tapes. I urgently put in the camcorder a DV tape where I filmed in *night shot* Anissa dancing naked on Dalida, a little gift for those who will analyze the digital tape. I can imagine the shock! They had to play it on a giant screen! In loop !

Last burst of vivacity: I put my laptop inside the comforter. It contains account numbers, *e-mail* addresses, photos and, above all, five hundred telephone numbers. The rookies' talent obliges, it has never been found. Quickly, I arrange the comforters and sheets, in bulk. Anissa, naked, lies on the bed for a long time. Thank you, darling!

Our stress is easing. We know what is going to happen, but we have taken care of it in less than an hour. The cops had to go get a locksmith. The ceramic of the overheated hot tub explodes.

I look through a corner of the curtain: no marshal in sight. I go back to bed to make love one last time.

My room has a counterpart: the *living room* of Hung's loft, where a lot of small toys are still made. Without being seen, I can see blue caps staring at my room but they can't see us. I guess that the rue Saint-Honoré is not the only place to be searched. I imagine that the same fate awakens the rue de Seine, the César workshop, Saint-Paul, the galleries of the Fleming and the auctioneers' offices that I knew. The magic collapses. The *dark* is announced for an undetermined time but which will be long, very long, undoubtedly. My social elevator went up too fast. The one that was never supposed to come back down was undermined. Free fall guaranteed. The cables of my staff and business have failed.

Allergic to ambition in the art world, I remain humble. My emotions are variable geometry, unstable and on *stand-by, now*. My biggest fear at the moment? That, because of the smoke, the firemen will come. They would be the only ones missing! Too bad, I have something else to think about: Anissa and I make love until 9:30 am, when the locksmith opens my armored door. The cops come in, still not sure they've found us. They have requisitioned two sworn witnesses to witness the search, in case no one was there.

They still thought the *flat* was empty! I'm happy with our subterfuge: three hours saved to destroy a maximum of evidence... and have a good time.

As soon as they enter my private museum, my alcove of celebration and love, the superheroes stammer out their fury: how? we didn't deign to answer their summons? I am laughing. 6 am is the legal time for them; for us, it makes no sense.

And then I look at the blues. I look at them in depth, blue-condensed, green blues of rage, the cerulean blues; and I think of Oscar de la Renta who imposed this color to high fashion. If he saw how much his color is overused, declining on the face of the marshals, sometimes gray because of the lack of UV! Other faces of blue appear to me green-red, and I think of Van Gogh, and I remember his correspondence with his brother Theo: he explains that to put side by side a green and a red flat allows him to express passion - oh human madness!

These cops, I will call them from now on "optical illusions", the Ï.O. They throw themselves at me, and I find myself flat on my back, in a bathrobe from the Carlton Hotel, handcuffed firmly behind my back. When my gaze falls on them, I observe their color palette and look for which of them has the most attractive color, the one best suited to their madness. Powerless, I attend this pitiful spectacle of polychromatic Ï.O. searching in an anarchic way, crossing and colliding. One of them reminded me of Godard, of the New Wave, of a blue not yet on sale in tubes; others just remind me of the blue Canard WC...

I am the spectator of my spoliation; the Ï.O. awkwardly unhook my works of art. They carry me into the living room like a madman or a dead animal. They throw me on the sofa. My conditioning has begun. I observe them bitterly, these Ï.O., released in my museum. They are having the time of their lives. It tears my heart out to see the hatred with which they take over the works in my collection.

When the Ï.O. enter the room, Anissa, always hot, gets up, lascivious creature of dreams, playing them the great charm of the *warm-up*. This diverts the blue minds on her and the unique spectacle of this rare beauty. Their expressions let sweat with big drops a not dissimulated envy. As a result, my dear bimbo slowly gets dressed.

Eventually, the O.I. let her go. I got carried away, arguing that she doesn't know anything, and that was enough for them. Relieved and happy, I have just enough time to kiss her one last time, then she disappears. She knows what she has to do, once she's out the door. She has most of my cell phone numbers on hers. We need to warn the fine folks who wouldn't be drowned in blue yet! In addition to seeing my sweetheart leave, probably for an eternity, I see my beloved works disappear before my eyes. I had started collecting since the age of fifteen. Farewell, my Picassos, my real Caesars - compressions and drawings! Farewell to the paintings of Frida Khalo and Diego Rivera! Farewell, my Miró on paper, my Botero bronze representing a nude of a coated woman! Farewell, my Cocteau drawings and my Hasegawa engravings! Strangely enough, they leave some of them behind - perhaps they have no more room in the vans they sent to rob me. There are a few personal works but also pieces by Rodin, Warhol, Cocteau, Venet, Arman, Wesselmann, Lichtenstein, César, real or fake - some of the compressions of children's cars are still scattered on the *living room* floor -, works by young artists, photos retouched on Photoshop, portraits of my wife Cïara-Ira, as well as a hundred or so authentic splendors.

The result of the shopping: the Ï.O. seize the equivalent of about two million euros worth of artworks that I loved. My heart is torn out. I am appalled, knotted, collapsed to see what I had created, accumulated, my pleasures, my happiness, my freedom, gone. My memories, the spirit of my works, the conditions in which I kept them, everything represents sweet endless moments attached to my love life. The rookies didn't just steal my property. They desecrated my museum and violated my privacy.

33. My interrogation period [September 2001]

Suffering and despair take hold of me as I see my life and its components being torn apart piece by piece. Surrounded by about fifteen bruises, I endure a trying interrogation. The questions and answers are done without me. I am a thousand miles away from their delirium and their speculations. They are on their own. Their stories? It's not my life. Anyway, these guys wouldn't know a postcard from a contemporary work; what are they waiting for? For me to give them a course in art history?

Failing to get a revelation out of me about anything important, they want to prove that they know us well from having followed us. So they tell me about our bimbos and the parties they would have liked to attend!

To my great astonishment, I was transferred to Seine-Saint-Denis, precisely in the gymnasium of a barracks. The Republican Guard was rehearsing there. What a *fight*, drums and trumpets *versus* techno and *rock and roll*! The objective of this relocation: to spread out on the floor all the works taken from the homes searched, to label them and attribute them to the different owners. Hundreds of pieces, digital material, legal documents and a lot of other things without the slightest interest are gathered.

I realize that the blues have also gathered here twenty or so respondents, in different rooms. There is my brother Franck, Pat Veinard, Christian Martin, Guy Pieters, Stéphanie Busuttil, Denyse Durand-Ruel, Khaled Ayari, Patrick Memoun, as well as many other gallery owners and collectors. For nearly thirty hours, all these people are questioned and harassed. Only Jean-Charles Villa, Yael Marciano and Laurent Strouck are missing. Good for them!

After having remained silent, dead tired, I signed the seals of the works that I recognized as being mine so that they could be returned to me later. It took me nine years to obtain this partial restitution: for the most beautiful pieces, Audrey Vazzana - my very subtle, delicate and forceful lawyer from Nice - had to go to appeal in order to win the case. In doing so, she gave me back my life and a priceless happiness, because each work I own has its own story. A story of love, of passions, of tears, of cracks, of loss of dear friends...

In the batch, there is also the result of my work of painter divided between two kinds of creation. The first kind is linked to my lovers. I coated their bodies with paint and then molded them on crystal paper that I then peeled off. It was an anthropometry of my lover-bodies, on the scale of love. The blues also carried a second kind of work of my hand: very large collages and cuttings of documents, photos and texts, questioning religion and its hypocrisy.

At the end of the legal period of custody, I find myself with Christian Martin. We are alone and chained, in the gaols of the Palais de l'Injustice in Bobigny. During these forty-eight hours - an eternity - that the blueprints steal from me, I have neither the right to consult a doctor, nor the right to feed myself. I sleep on a kind of rotten mattress, on the floor, like a dog; and I think of James Baldwin, desperate for the world and its puppets, who had given me his cult book, illustrating so well this treatment that is sometimes inflicted on certain human beings: *Less than a dog...*

34. My Fresnes period
[October 2001]

When the rookies are done with their barrage of questions, we leave Bobigny to be thrown into a bottomless pit: Fresnes prison. There is no way to wash off the filth that now surrounds us, forming a deep-sea diving suit; each second lasts forever and repeats itself like a Philip Glass formula. Later, we are again transported into the unknown. Here we are on our way to Grasse, in order to appear, in our trampy state, before the examining magistrate Thierry Laurent.

I am aware that I look like a bear coming out of its cave in a rage, ice age. Christian Martin is wearing his usual war *reporter*'s outfit. He reminds me of a hostage who has escaped from his captors but got lost in a deep forest, without a compass. His white hair, curled in an afro, seems to want to escape into space and to flee from the round face of a child fed on cereals and McDonald's.

How far away I seem to be from night landings in a Learjet, with red carpet and dark glasses, between Milan, Ibiza, Paris, Tokyo, New York, Shanghai! *Forget that*, Eric! *Game over*! We are carried around by six specialized gendarmes, as if we were terrorists, dangerous beings when (or because?) we have no cause to defend, except that of the love of art and creativity. The TGV takes us to Cannes. We are not allowed to eat, drink or go to the bathroom. At

179

the administrative lunch time, each gendarme, between two jokes, crunches in his sandwich and drinks a beer, without realizing that they are humiliating us. It's too much: I ask for a drink noisily, so that the travelers can hear me. I have money, I can pay; but I am ready to go to drink the water (not drinkable) of the toilets.

The rookies stop stuffing themselves and realize that they have forgotten us. Alas, instead of allowing us to buy food and water, they just pack up their picnic. *Standing ovation* for selfishness!

We arrive at the courthouse in Grasse without having been able to smoke.

A little compensation, then: I have the pleasure of seeing Patrick Luciani arrive, my friend from the big parties, a brilliant defender; he is there, with the lawyers who have come from Paris to defend the hostage Christian Martin. Patrick explains to me that the situation is contrasted: on the principle, it is not brilliant; in reality, the judge does not have many elements to oppose us. To my great surprise, in my cell, I received a visit from the dean of the investigating judges, who was respectful, to say the least. A rare occurrence in the history of justice and relations between prisoners and judges, he left his office to comfort me in a low voice. He begs me to hold on, saying that he appreciates me a lot... and yet, it is this gentleman who had investigated the case of the false Chagall and Miró in 1985! His courtesy touches me. The morale goes up a little.

While Patrick compiles the file, I rest on a concrete bench. For me, it is as soft as a futon, I am so *dead*. If Japan is the country of the rising sun, Grasse and its jails are the country of dying misery!

When the examining magistrate finally summoned me to his office, he received me in the proper manner. For all that, I have nothing more to say to him than to the gendarmes. On the other hand, his questions enlighten me. I quickly learned that, of all the people searched in Paris, Saint-Paul and in Europe, we were the fourth to be heard. Guy Pieters and my brother Franck were interviewed the day before. The judge decided to leave Franck alone. He asked that his money be returned to him (my brother had the equivalent of 30,000 € in *cash* on him!) and ordered that he be set free, much to the displeasure of the blue.

Guy Pieters was almost as lucky as he was. Green with fear but rich with millions, he cried so much that he was able to get out by paying a bail equivalent to 150 000 e, drawing his checkbook in the very second when the judge considered letting him free on bail. He was thus able to go back to his activities, after the seizure of the few Caesars that were in Saint-Paul. Stéphanie Busuttil was heard for more than thirty hours in the premises of the research section. She denied any participation in the traffic, she delivered explanations which satisfied provisionally the judge Laurent. She came out of custody free. Good for her!

Denyse Durand-Ruel had to explain the presence of fake Caesars with real certificates and real archive numbers. She argued that she had only included works in the catalog raisonné because she had been convinced of their authenticity by someone close enough to Caesar to support her feeling. The expert in question denied any fraud. Denyse Durand-Ruel denied having used Guy Pieters to appraise the disputed pieces, but she confirmed that Stéphanie had established, apparently in good faith, certificates of authentication for certain disputed pieces. For the judges, the enigma is not ready to dissipate!

Christian Martin admitted everything, and more if necessary: among other things, he admitted to have provided the stamps of Caesar's thumbprint and the stamps of the Beaux-arts workshop; he admitted that he interceded to obtain certificates of authenticity from Stéphanie Busuttil and others, in order to give them to LøL, Pat, Pieters and all those concerned... except me! He gave up all his entourage, his family, Giacobetti, Caesar's portrait photographer, as well as Perrin, the guardian of the Busuttil-Caesar temple. He directed suspicions towards certain galleries, such as that of the sulphurous Anne Lettrée. For his sentence, he left charged but free, trembling with all his neurons - or at least, with what was left of them.

The questions kept coming down on me. The examining magistrate questioned me at length about the theft of paintings from the Retelet gallery in Saint-Paul, in May 2001. In view of the wiretaps, he told me that I would probably be dismissed from the case of the theft. However, the César affair is consecutive to the complaint for theft of three paintings, a case that does not concern me. Strange as well as strange...

Immediately, I remember my meeting with Retelet, in August 2001. I was in Saint-Tropez with some friends. We were celebrating when I received a surprising phone call from this gallery owner. He managed to get my cell phone number from one of my ex-girlfriends in Vence, under a ridiculous pretext. He invites me to join him at his gallery. I accepted the invitation, leaving Saint-Tropez and its pleasures behind for a day. On the spot, the dealer receives me in his office in a confidential way. He asks me if I know about the theft of four paintings from his gallery: a small Chagall, *L'Emigrant*, which was supposedly to be sold a few days later; a *Partie de plaisir*, the title said it all, which was also about to be sold; a very ugly Fernand Léger and a more or less correct Magritte. Value of the lot: the equivalent of 750 000 €. I say that if I hear of anything, I'll come back to him; however, given my busy (and ultra-successful) life, it's unlikely that I'll hear of anything.

Retelet admits to me that he is more than annoyed because he is not insured and will have to reimburse his client. He shows me the photos and the certificates of the stolen works. This detail makes me wonder: the thieves did not recover the certificates; in other words, the works are not really resellable, except at ridiculous prices. Another disturbing detail: the quality of these works leaves something to be desired. Perplexed but good-natured, I offered to help him and left him three Caesar's boxes containing crushed little cars. He only has to sell them to make money; I am not in a hurry to be paid. The authenticated Caesars didn't cost me much; I had so many that I could leave him some to get by.

What he forgot to tell me, and what I learned from Judge Laurent, is that the theft was already four months old, and that, when he filed his complaint, he had, by chance, declared to the gendarmerie that I was a regular in his gallery, as well as other friends who used to make fake Caesars with me. He specified that he had seen my vehicle the night of the theft, which is ridiculous. As a result of this denunciation, we were wiretapped for four months between May 21 and September 27, 2001. Because of this banal theft in a gallery, I was followed, as well as all the protagonists of the affair: gallery owners, collectors, César's entourage and night companions. The gendarmes filmed us compressing in Grasse and compensating during nights of debauchery. I laughed while imagining their hours of tailing, from Man Ray to the VIP, to the Barfly, to Cathy Guetta's, magical nights *non stop*! I imagined them jealous of us and therefore cursing us. Some rookies spoke to me later, in private, about all these *jet set stars*; they had *printed* them in their heads and kept them under their caps!

On the one hand, the investigators were delighted to go from a theft of paintings to a vast traffic of forgeries appraised by the rightful owners. On the other hand, they have a problem: no one complained about buying fake Caesars. Without a complaint, there was no trafficking in forgeries - and for good reason, all our buyers had only authenticated works!

Nevertheless, this story of theft intrigued me because the stolen works were unsaleable for at least four reasons: they were ugly; they did not correspond to any key period for the artists; they were of more than mediocre quality; and they had been taken without their certificates. Yet these were the only pieces that were stolen after being loaned by collectors for Retelet to sell. Even once in the place, the thieves would have ignored Retelet's personal collection, which includes high-quality Mirós (with their certificates), Magrittes, Warhols, Basquiat, Alechinskys, all of which are worth five times as much as the missing near-crops.

Let's be clear: for me, this affair smells bad. And I am even more angry at Retelet for having dragged me through the mud, for having involved me in this masquerade and for nailing me to the pillory of infamy. Alone. Worn out, tired, almost dead. Without his stab in the back, the Caesar affair would have had a different ending, I imagine. This Retelet is at the root of all my misfortunes. On arrival, I was the only one to be taken to the Nice prison, charged and imprisoned. *Flight* to hell!

35. My period in Nice
[October 2001]

In the prison of Nice, I am thrown into a hole subjected to agitations of all kinds. Screams, prisoners degrading their cell while screaming, prisoners playing techno music at full blast on their powerful stereo, a noisy and disturbing mix. I find myself in the company of a Chechen pimp and an Italian *coke* dealer. They hallucinate when they see me entering their cave. They look at me, in an *uncool* way. I take the lead and ask if there is a problem. The guys reassure me: everything is fine, they are just surprised to see me when I have just been on TV. So they let me have the top bunk, the one closest to the kind of window. There, I can breathe better and even see the starry sky. For two days, I sleep. No medicine, no food. Just cigarettes that my fellow inmates generously offer me. They must feel that I am taken by anguish, invaded by hatred to find myself there because of a theft of which I am innocent! Moreover, I guess that the investigation of the false-true Caesars will be very, very long. Too many protagonists in Europe, Asia and the United States. The investigators must compare, over several years, the works sold and those that have disappeared from the Caesar estate, of which they have neither photos nor formal descriptions! I'm not a blue-blood. I have been convicted in the past, several times. Except that I knew how long I was going to be away. I've never done a potentially infinite amount of pre-trial, or custody, in a case of this magnitude.

To make matters worse, the weather is still nice. I think of libertine pleasures, of the sea, of parties, of *beautiful people* having fun in Ibiza and Saint-Tropez, without me. I can't even write to them. I am censored, walled up, isolated, incommunicado, without a private room. From time to time, they bring me a bag of clean clothes that one of my friends left at the front door of this misery box.

My fellow inmates are the only ones I interact with. I kill time by playing chess with the proxo. Only my anxiety attacks provoke a dialogue with the tortured person that I am.

In this cell, I feel the microwave effect. A window of one meter by fifty centimeters lets in the minimum vital air for three prisoners. I live H24 in a niche of 9 m² for three. Mosquitoes, surely emigrated from Transylvania and therefore globules-addicts, dare to venture here to pump me what remains of my blood. The slamming of the locks of our cell doors haunt me. If a man's greatness is not measured in moments of comfort but in times of adversity, this is the time to test me.

I don't go out in the unbreathable courtyards. I stay locked in my cage. I don't want to mingle with a hundred people in 100 m² of space. Gone is the blue sky of Klein that protected my life. The azure has mixed with the deep black. I take advantage of the fact that my fellow inmates go jogging to meditate, to dream, to get out of this impasse. The only air I breathe is made of nicotine and dust. During my few hours of solitude, I do a little washing and try to remove the dirt that covers me.

Time becomes abstract. I am afraid of going crazy and paranoid. I suffocate, the TV stays on, without sound. It is the only window that speaks to me from outside. The reflections of the screen projected on the walls send back to me yellows, blues, red in abstract movement.

A dilemma tortures me. Should I put an end to my days and to these eternal nights, stop this time which is no longer moving and which I suspend thanks to handfuls of sleeping pills stocked in industrial quantities that I gobble up permanently? Or should I fight, with all the forces I can muster, for example to denounce these inhuman treatments which break the weakest, humiliate the naive and frighten the simplest? These fundamental failures to respect dignity become my fight. Supported by Master Vazzana, I rally to this cause the journalists of the national press, of the television, of Canal Plus, including the team of Karl Zéro. To give me courage, I think back to what the lawyer Thierry Lévy said:

- Our heads are harder than prison walls!

My lawyer comes every day. It's the only visit I have the right to. We take the opportunity to answer questions asked by *Le Point* or *Libération*, among others. My deplorable conditions of incarceration, my lack of medication are now in the public eye. I informed the director in person. He thanked me for telling him and asked me what I needed urgently. I give him a complete list. He grants me everything I want. My frankness and the fear of being the target of the media had their little effect! So, I get the authorization to go to the library. I borrowed art books, about Zao Wou-Ki in particular. I enroll in the prison art class, where I help the brave volunteer to make herself understood by the prisoners who want to draw and model. I bring to my partners a little of my knowledge. The time passes more quickly. I take the opportunity to get brushes, Indian ink, tubes of paint, sheets of paper. Life takes back colors.

In the meantime, my combative lawyer filed a complaint with the European Court of Human Rights for non-assistance to a person in danger. Earthquake within the cave, the prosecutors, the judges, the press and the opinion - scandalized but impotent!

These prisons are like biatchs in *gang bangs*. Some inmates enter them by force, several times, come out and return in recidivism; then others take over in all directions by the big door and come out by the small one, free, leaving their place to these insatiable people, all on a crowded plateau. Between the stars of this sad pornography, the suicides who did not resist - and they are legion -, and the sons of the air who make me regret not having invested my money in Eurocopter shares, choose your side, comrade! Other people are going crazy, if they weren't before. They express themselves by bellowing, fighting to know that they exist, for nothing... Others still, suffering from Gilles de la Tourette syndrome, speak alone and shout their insults into the void that does not hear them. Overcrowding, dilapidation, promiscuity... Morality: we can only observe that the investigating judges use and abuse pre-trial detention. It is one of their favorite rituals. May the indignation gain ground in front of the appalling factory of recidivism that constitutes the French prison.

However, it has been two centuries since, under the influence of Montesquieu, humanists and hygienists began to plead for a healing and not only punitive confinement. Since then, reports have been piling up. The first one, on a European scale, was written in 1777 by the Englishman John Howard, trying to articulate social vengeance and the need for reinsertion. Many claim to be reforming, while in fact they are hastening to repress. The media, which constantly rediscovers the reality of prisons, thus starts a new cycle: exaltation of the reform, repressive reversal and then oblivion! This is still the case today: we know that prisons are overcrowded, euphemism; the politicians who spend (briefly) under the bars are offended by this; we listen to them, then, for lack of courage, it falls back.

Luckily, I have enough money to buy my food, much to the delight of my fellow inmates. I cook Italian. They send me important money orders. I start to breathe again. Especially since I have to admit that, as a forger, I have always been respected in prison by the kings, the wardens and even the directors, with whom I spent hours talking about painting, an art they practiced as amateurs while waiting to retire. So much the worse if, internally, I laughed at the thought of the scabs for which they spent so much energy and which represented lousy subjects! I was on the verge of laughter when they showed me their rotten work. I felt sorry for their brushes - no doubt they would have preferred to lose their hair - and for their colors, which would have gladly returned to their respective tubes rather than be humiliated.

I take advantage of my precaution to make about a hundred drawings by César and a dozen by Zao Wou-Ki, for fun. I learn to know better this Chinese artist still alive today. I will leave with all these drawings and inks, but when? Answer: January 8, 2002. The judge gives me back my car. I also ask for the return of everything that is not Caesar's, except for a few works that were sold to me or exchanged about fifteen years ago. From my cell, I take only my drawings by César and Zao Wou-Ki. The rest I leave to my two fellow inmates. Goodbye, and forever!

36. My "advice to an expat" period [January 2002]

When I left the cave in Nice, the media asked me for dozens of interviews. Among the curious, Jean-Michel Verne, a direct descendant of Jules Verne. The result of his questions, published in the *Vrai journal* papier, will be called "20 000 leagues under the sea of art". Around me, it is madness. The press gets carried away, asserts that a thousand forgeries of Caesar would have been certified for tens of millions of euros. They claim that Caesar is less brilliant than his forger. I am not fooled. Forgeries have never frightened the art world but, genius being rare, they try to convince the gogos that only genius forgers manage to make an illusion. From then on, all slightly gifted forgers become "genius" when, inspired by the spirit of the master, they manage to drape themselves in the same aura.

This nonsense doesn't change anything to my reality: I am under house arrest on the French Riviera with a ban to leave the Alpes-Maritimes. So I invite my friends and concubines there, to kill with them this time of free imprisonment. I party for three months because, in winter as in summer, there is nothing better to do in Saint-Paul.

With the agreement of the judge, I end up going back to Paris, leaving this coast of usury that I could never bear in high doses.

Business picked up. I start writing this book, and I replenish my finances by selling Caesar and Zao Wou-Ki to the same customers as before. Surreal! I get back in touch with my three friends who have not been heard by the police: Jean-Charles Villa, who has taken refuge in Bali; Pat Veinard, in the castle he bought for himself thanks to the fake Caesars; and my friend Yaël Marciano, who has been by my side since the beginning, for business as well as for parties. I told the judge that Yael did not know that these were fake paintings that I was selling or that he was selling for me. This saved her from an immediate indictment.

The funny thing is that, two days before our arrests, Martin, Yael and I had an appointment with Guy Pieters to finalize some transactions. I had called Yaël to warn him that we would be paid, two or three days later, the equivalent of 600 000 €. Yaël answered that we would go to a mega party at that time. In the meantime, he is in the suburbs with his family to prepare Yom Kippur. On September 27, 2001, it is the day of the great forgiveness. Everything is turned off, Yael is unreachable. We still laugh about it. He will be questioned only on June 24, 2003 and will declare that *big fiestas* were organized in Paris, in Europe and on the coast. The paintings? The sculptures? Pfff, he doesn't know anything about them...

While in Paris, LøL gave me an appointment at the Marly café, an establishment with a view on the Peï pyramid, in the middle of the square courtyard of the Louvre. He wants us to arrange our versions for the day when he will be arrested - because he managed to escape to Dubai, to the Burjalarab hotel, *the place to be*, the day after the arrests. He sent me a very charming text message when you know what happened to me: "New life under better auspices...". He set up a company in the Emirates free zone. He works directly with the sons of Sheikh Al Maktoum, who rules his emirate with an iron fist. Times are hard for his people, but not for foreigners who bring ideas and, above all, money! LøL had important contacts with the Minister of Finance to open a modern art museum; conceptual, this remained at the project stage.

Today, he can no longer stand the climate of Dubai, torn between a freezing atmosphere at night and the fifty degrees of the day, dispensed by a sun that melts his spirit. He feels obliged to live reclusively in his air-conditioned palace, and he can't take it anymore. So LøL leaves Dubai for Bali, a surfer's paradise. He only has the equivalent of €300,000 to live on, and in Bali, life for the rich is not so expensive. Friendly atmosphere, superb villa that he rents with domesticity, pool, forest and tropical park. The atmosphere is festive and glamorous, between two surf spots where he spends the day riding the waves. He organizes *trashy* sex parties with Balinese and Thai girls and extreme surfing freaks coming from all over to have fun. It doesn't change him much from our Parisian lives, but it's a lot more sporty!

He tells me that a few days before the arrest, Retelet would have told him that the business was hot-burning-dangerous and that he had to flee. Retelet had the magnificent Ferrari compressed and put it up for sale at Cornette de Saint-Cyr. Prominently featured in the catalog of a contemporary art sale, it was sold for the equivalent of €100,000, and his share was transferred to one of LøL's accounts. The piece was seized in October 2001, along with the authentication certificates. At the end of our meeting, this fake brother advised me to stop everything on the Caesars. Thank you, LøL, you impress me!

For many weeks, I had no more *news from* Jean-Charles. I learn, from friends of his, that he continues his Bali-Paris-Bali round trips, and that he works (one must live) on fake works of Robert Combas, Fernand Léger and Chagall! I also know that he was introduced by Christine-the-revenger to the Balinese princess Jaïs Darga Widjawa. LøL will push his professional conscience to the point of becoming her lover long enough to sell her forgeries wit-

36. MY "ADVICE TO AN EXPAT" PERIOD [JANUARY 2002]

hout certificates. According to the princess, LøL was her romance. She owned Darga galleries all over Far East Asia and sold in abundance, laundering the dirty money of the mafia-triads who had huge amounts of capital to transform. Thanks to the princess, LøL made millions of dollars. Enough to make himself look good before dumping his benefactress!

I saw LøL again at the Marly café in September 2002. He continued to produce new Modiglianis, "Women with long necks" that he had already done and sold well. As he had learned to make Braques and all sorts of Combas, he repeated himself until he was worn out. He had clients in Andorra and the French Senate. Eager to diversify, he will realize, in the style of the narrative Figuration, the "crime scenes" which are the reflection and the spirit of the own staging of the plastic artist Jacques Monory. All these works, realized in Bali, will be, thanks to his political and *jet set* relations, resold in the open. The senator-collectors are not very careful with their pleasures, especially with the taxpayers' money!

So when I saw him again, LøL had added a few million euros to his portfolio. On leaving our meeting, he flew to Bali *via* Amsterdam. There was an emergency: the libertine forger had to find his young Thai concubine who was about to give birth to her son!

Shortly afterwards, by cell phone, I advise LøL not to set foot on French soil again. He replies that he will stay in Asia with his newborn son but that he will go to Andorra by roundabout ways to sell some Mirós, major works on canvas, mixed media, to his banker and to the curator of the Miró museum in Barcelona. He's really good at it! On the other hand, when LøL asks me for *news* about the César affair, I only answer him a few words: "To be avoided! Too *hot*!"

37. My omerta period [December 2002]

While sitting at the terrace of the Flore, I receive a phone call from my lawyer. She asks me to read the December 3, 2002 edition of *Libération*. The César affair is back in the news because Jean-Charles Villa was arrested on his return from Bali. LøL goes directly from Roissy to Grasse, in the office of Judge Laurent. Thanks to the arrest of this second copyist, who describes himself as my pupil, the investigators now count a large thousand certified false Caesars, half of which have been seized, the other half safely stored in private collections around the world.

LøL does not mention the gallery owners, collectors and sponsors. Faced with the evidence, he acknowledges that Stéphanie Busuttil has certified a number of works at the request of Christian Martin and himself; and he adds that, perhaps, some certificates have been issued erroneously. "Perhaps"! Nevertheless, this is not what the investigators are primarily interested in. Indeed, according to what LøL will tell me, the quantities of works sold are such that the investigators prefer to look at the distribution channels. The rich collectors not being gogos, the investigators think of a circuit of money laundering that they estimate at about twenty million euros.

They are not wrong. The astronomical sums of money that we are left with in exchange for considerable works and orders are indeed dirty money. Filtered through various gambling casinos in Europe, this barely laundered money is available to the bulk of our buyers. Hence the ever-increasing demand for major works. These works, bought by *offshore* companies, in the most complete anonymity, spend some time in the safes of various free ports, just like the majority of mine; then they are put back on the art market, under the cover of *offshore* companies. Dirty money is thus dry cleaned by the art dry cleaner, capable of washing more white than ultra-white!

Artists have always paid with their lives for the possibility to be free and to put their colors on white canvases. What makes a work of art beautiful is the way we look at it and the way it was executed, with passion, love, rage, violence, emotion. The Greeks had the cult of the body, of beauty, of aestheticism; this heritage is still alive. Beauty is a form of intelligence, thought Oscar Wilde. My artistic piracy did not kill nor ruin anybody, on the contrary; but I missed a thousand times to kill myself by playing the doubloons without lining. I risked my life by creating this diabolical mixture of real and fake, by developing my propensity to ridicule laws, legislators and magistrates thanks to my nonchalant and detached attitude, in short, by displaying my sense of provocation behind which I try to hide a sickly timidity. My shamelessness conceals, as much as it succeeds, the extreme modesty that characterizes me.

Whether or not they are morally condemned, my practices hit the nail on the head. More: each participant has blessed them. In this immense traffic of false works of art, all - heirs, holders of the moral rights, experts, merchants and art lovers - closed their eyes and put their hands to the work. The hydra I created served many private interests. The transactions of the César affair were settled in cash and involved tens of millions of euros. I got rich, certainly; above all, I enriched many people who, for their part, remain beyond the reach of justice - the law of silence prevails in this kind of *business*.

Since the 1980's, I have made thousands of forgeries that have been bought, sold, resold, forgotten, and have fed the banks of *offshore* havens. Today, the megabenefits of the buyers are safe in the banks, UBS in Geneva, HSBC in Lausanne, Carnegie Bank in Luxembourg, Republic Bank of New York in Monaco, ex-Bank Bacob in Brussels, Credit Suisse in Geneva... and especially in the casinos of Knokke!

The little drug addict-sick person who lived in me could not imagine such a result obtained thanks to an energy drawn I don't know where, perhaps in a crazy desire to live and to play this easy game.

In this Shakespearian fight for the control of the international art market of Caesar's work, of the false interpretations but perfectly in the spirit of the master, all authenticated by the best experts, we were the center, the inexhaustible source where all the *art's addict collectors* drank greedily. We enriched the already very rich collectors and gallery owners. We never robbed or ruined anyone. We have never had any complaints, only requests! The proof: the cops have not found anyone serious to be a civil party and this, *all over the planet of art*! On his umpteenth return from Bali, LøL did not think he was wanted. Unluckily, he was incarcerated and put under investigation. He was released free but under judicial supervision.

He didn't say anything about the others, just saying that I had taught him everything. The César affair will not break the *omerta* that reigns in the art market.

38. My Zao Wou-Ki period [2003]

During the affair, the business continues. The César family is fighting. A sale was cancelled *in extremis*. The State got involved and got tangled up, renouncing its tax reassessment of the master's widow thanks to the intervention of Éric Woerth, Minister of Finance, who was sensitive to pressure from Alain-Dominique Perrin, a major donor to the UMP. For the same reasons, the number of "missing" works was drastically reduced, which provoked the fury of the Baldaccini clan. Intrigued by these upheavals, Karl Zéro devoted an hour of his *Vrai journal* to me, which was then in full swing.

Other cases are solved. Thus, on January 31, 2005, an anonymous informant revealed to the gendarmes of Lons-le-Saunier that the three works stolen from Retelet's house four years earlier were in the hands of gypsies from the Grenoble region, among whom was a certain Loulou, identified as Louis Benoni. Immediately, the rookies put Benoni under surveillance. It appears that he has ongoing relationships with Stéphane Bauza, a truck driver, and Daniel Mokhfi, a secondhand dealer in possession of beautiful paintings from the Midi. Finally, on March 21, 2005, the two main suspects of the Retelet Gallery robbery were arrested. A search of Mokhfi's garage revealed three of the four paintings stolen from Saint-Paul, hidden in garbage bags or cardboard boxes: *L'Emigrant* by Chagall, *L'Écuelle et le tire-bouchon* by Léger, and *Jour de fête* by Magritte. The three accomplices were about to resell the merchandise.

Even today, I still hate these three men, but even more so the Retelet gallery. I can't get it out of my mind that I am now a broke man, a starving man because of this Nickel Pieds affair! Since my release from prison in 2002, I have lived almost exclusively from the sale of my accumulated savings abroad as well as from forgeries, which I continue to manufacture in very small quantities. For the anecdote, my landlord at the time, on rue Saint-Honoré, accepted to be paid in Zao Wou-Ki inks. He explained to me that it was for his nephews and grandchildren, for later on. He is a *fan*!

I am fascinated by this fabulous Chinese artist, who settled in Paris in the late 1940s. His work is fine, abstract, sensual, delicate. To prolong it, I create small format China inks, on Canson paper previously yellowed in very strong tea. On the soaked or almost dry paper, I dip my Chinese brushes in the ink and let, in the manner of this great artist and therefore at the mercy of a very undirected chance, this almost untamable ink slide. For fear of missing my finished ink by spoiling the signature in Chinese, I first undertook to learn it and then to draw it first, with the Sergent Major pen, on the blank sheets.

Happy to have mastered a little Chinese, I made a hundred of them. I take about thirty of them to present them to art dealers and galleries on the rue de Seine such as the Lebouc gallery, to whom I had sold lithographs by Miró and Chagall, as well as ceramics by Picasso. The son Lebouc buys some of them from me and pays me in cash. I am satisfied. Other dealers buy pieces from me at knock-down prices. So much the worse. The main thing for me is to earn enough to support myself and my partner Li Lavilliers - the former third wife of the great Bernard.

In 2009, already under indictment and imprisoned in the Grasse prison, I was interviewed by police officers in charge of investigating forgeries of Zao Wou-Ki's work. The procedure is initiated by an examining magistrate of the financial division of Paris.

I acknowledge the facts and am taken by plane to Paris. There I met this investigating judge, who was very friendly. She is relevant, very kind and surrounded by a quantity of books on this Chinese artist. She confided to me that, thanks to me, she had discovered the artist and learned to love him. As for my works, she liked them... but not the rightful owners of the Zao Wou-Ki Foundation! So she charged me, and I was tried at the Tribunal de Grande Instance de Marseille. Here I am, a resident of the iconic Baumettes prison! Sentenced to two years in prison, I do not appeal: my sentence will be confused with the one that the Tribunal de Grande Instance of Grasse will impose on me for the César case.

39. The trial [December 2009]

On November 30, 2009, the César trial opened, eight years after the events. However, time and oblivion have done their work. Moreover, some of the protagonists are absent because the instructions have cleared them, in particular our great fellow Pat Veinard, as his nickname indicates. Good for them! On the other hand, nine other forgers (including Christian Martin, my brother Franck, Jean-Charles Villa and Yaël Marciano), gallery owners (Anne Lettrée, Laurent Strouk, Patrick Memoune, Guy Pieters), and amateurs are on my side. As experts, Denyse Durand-Ruel and Stéphanie Busuttil are civil parties, although the latter has acknowledged having appraised some twenty or thirty works. Despite the evidence, I am happy for them. What's done is done, it's no longer up to me to blame anyone.

On the first day, I am in pole position, drowned by the court under a flood of questions based on statements, mine and those of my accomplices - phony, untruthful and unverifiable statements. Since 2001, we have been more or less on the same wavelength. So the court is looking for loopholes, in vain. It dreams of a movie studio light to illuminate truths and to make the organization chart of the participation of each of my accomplices; all it diffuses is a wolfish light whose halo is penumbra, between dog and wolf.

The mediocrity of a botched investigation as well as the procedural errors raised by our lawyers disrupt the serenity of the debates. I am the only one incarcerated. I am more and more sick, tired, stressed, mistreated, handcuffed tightly behind my back, *up side down*, serial forger surrounded by four Robocops who jostle me, lift me off the ground, mistreat me. I yell at them, ask them to treat me properly, and threaten them to reveal my conditions of detention when I am not in the sacrosanct room.

As I walk back and forth from the Baumettes jails to the courtroom, I think again of James Baldwin and *Less Than a Dog*. I am weakened, but my brain is working in overboosted mode. He and I have no room for error. In my toiletless, waterless jail, in the stench of shit, piss and vomit, I imagine the questions I'll be asked and the answers I'd better give. I am a chess player; it is exhausting, but I play big, and not only my fate! I want my free accomplices not to be implicated by a blunder that I could commit although the president, seasoned, asks questions in the disorder.

In these insalubrious jails, I am given almost nothing to eat - a bag of picnic food, a bag of chips, two cookies, a quart of water, and that's all. During these five days of judicial marathon, every morning, I am taken out of the cell at 7 am. I don't have time to take a shower, I hide some Lexomil in the hem of my pants, I quickly take my tritherapies. They take me from *speed* to the Palais jail. I am exhausted! The pressure of the debates, the interruptions that bring me back to this underground dungeon, until 9 or 10 am when I am pulled towards the courtroom... I re-enter the prison cell at 9 pm, I only have one desire, to sleep. I don't eat, I don't sleep, I wait for the slamming of the locks every moment of the night.

Back at the courthouse, I head for the cave where I bend over like a fetus to try to rest a little. With the light in my face, lying on this studded wooden bench, I twist and turn but can't find the Zen position. Every morning I am stripped naked and searched. It amuses them. I am suffocating. The stale air suffocates me. I read on the walls, which have the word, the insults engraved or blackened, the names of the defendants who passed long before me and who left a trace of their fifteen minutes of distress.

At 10 am, I enter the courtroom. Television cameras, photographers, *perchmen* harass me. Even though I don't look my best, I smile at them, I play the comedy they expect from me. As long as I'm doing this, I might as well be in the media! The scarlet Ï.O. untie me and try to put on a good face.

Since the first questions in 2001, I have always cleared my team. I am the one who had the idea of this set-up; I am the one who created this underground economy. I am the soul of this business. Yes, I have enriched all the protagonists who are with me in the dock - and a few others too; yes, I have enriched myself; however, above all, I have had fun building this game. I laugh when I hear that Busuttil and Durand-Ruel are asking for 15,000 € in compensation: I imagine that their lawyers have taken three times that amount in fees.

The disproportion between their demands and what we have earned is a form of admission on their part!

All my accomplices have been briefed: we must drown the fish, throw false responsibilities on each other that are purely and simply invented, put a firewall between the court and us, confuse them, make them forget the content of their file, play for time, smoke them out! Our masquerade has been working for eight years! Not seen, not taken! They want something heavy, we offer them something *light*! They will only get dumb fry! As a result, we are blamed for 150 fakes, while we have made thousands of them.

The smartest one is Guy Pieters. His lawyer invokes procedural errors. The court could only be seized of the facts between January 1 and August 31, 2001. Thus, the search of September

39. The trial [December 2009]

27, 2001 and the telephone tapping of September 6 and 19 must be excluded from the proceedings. Bravo, the Fleming!

On the second day of this messy and blackish trial, we were presented with a few fake Caesars. I can't think of a single one that I would have executed; it must be said that mine have been appraised and sold as real *all over the wide world*. In truth, I recognize the pattern... but LøL does not recognize anything. It's normal!

So who will the court award it to? That is the question! Motus-omerta on our side, in this ring where the art of the real is mixed with the art of the fake! A pleiad of legal experts, including Jean-Paul Ledeur, a friend of Caesar's, blithely reveal their incompetence. It is however to these *fakes*, all more ignorant than the others, that the Court asks unceasingly if these works are false and if the signatures are good. After hours spent touching them, analyzing them from the front and from the back, studying the assemblies, seeing if they are glued, screwed, nailed, smelling them, trying to feel Caesar's spirit coming out of them, these experts will not be able to pronounce themselves.

No, experts, you will not find anything illicit. Everything is true! LøL won and yet his works were very different from mine! It's over! No more blatant evidence! There is room for doubt in the minds of this court! No one will uncover our magic and the recipes of this *salsa*. To think that the world of truth and falsity depends on these clowns, ridiculous clowns making their ball with the circus of art and its trade... So we make a mockery of everything! Our lawyers jump at these non-evidences of falsity! They have the easy part, they benefit from it! Journalists smile at me with congratulations; some tell me that what we have done is genius. In reality, there is nothing genius. Just reflection, work and creation.

Third day, same circus. I'm down and out, getting worse and worse. For three days I have not eaten or showered. This is the real punishment! The court continues to harass me; in spite of my suffering, stoic, I remain standing and I answer. I lead them astray in a stream of irrelevant words, they listen to me. I am the *target* to whom they shoot arrows soaked in bitterness, mixed with sulphuric acid, whose expiration date has passed. It is me that one wants! Black dresses and *red monkeys* faces!

Mr. Vazzana points out that I do not have broad enough shoulders to bear the entirety of what I am accused of. Yes, I am a forger; but I am incapable of having implemented this perfect set-up alone! I don't wear Prada; in this case, I am the Sweet Devil! I am at the point where I sometimes burst out laughing, destabilizing the almost monastic atmosphere of this opera buffa.

To the twenty million euro turnover that I am accused of, I always answer the same thing:

- The IRS is too generous with its estimates, especially as Christmas approaches!

I am told that my trafficking was to support my extravagant lifestyle. I retort that I declare my taxes. Thus the 180 000 € served to the administration for the year 2000, representing my gains on cubist works of Picasso, impressionists, Monet and Renoir, sold to wealthy Asian customers whose names I will not reveal by discretion... and because they never existed! Let them send rogatory commissions to Korea, Malaysia, India, Hong Kong, Shanghai! Let them go to Macao to look for Mr. Chow, that's my dream! In short, I try to drown them in their own pond...

Last day of this circus face for the sodomite justice! The prosecutor's requisitions fall: six months suspended for my lucky co-defendants, four years firm for me. He could have asked for life imprisonment! As a bonus, this puppet asks us to pay taxes on unproven gains or, if they were, on *black money* generated by a fake traffic! That's nonsense!

The lawyers of my accomplices compete in ingenuity to dismantle the accusation. The files are dissected, exploded, torn to pieces, as well as the arguments of the carmine red prosecutor with a touch of lead green.

Maître Vazzana pleads last. She hits the nail on the head, short and simple, stating:

- There is no evidence that my client has put anything on the market that has not been authenticated by the leading experts in the field. He is not the only one to have collected and sold works by this great sculptor. My accomplices will come to embrace me and thank me for not having given them up. The judges will have tried in vain to fold me like an origami. On the other hand, I finish this trial flat, still blinded by the *flashes of* the photographers and the lamps of the cameras, drunk by the questions of the journalists of all the paper and TV presses. My message is straightforward:

- I liked Caesar, I had a good time. I'm moving on. Only art and love animate me and will continue to make me vibrate. Hi!

The trial is set for January 25, 2010. I am waiting for the decision from the bottom of my cave. Here, the jails are dirty, and the food is unhealthy. These conditions lead some prisoners to depression which, if not properly treated, leads to suicide! The French prison does not respect human beings, it crushes them. In front of me, a director told a prison officer that he was running a human waste reprocessing plant. Even today, we must fight against this dangerous and even deadly hypocrisy that scorns the dignity of tens of thousands of human beings.

At the end of a pitiful suspense, I was sentenced to four years in prison. Jean-Charles Villa gets three years with a detention order. Christian Martin gets two years suspended; Franck, Yaël and Laurent Strouck get one year suspended, the thieves get between one and three years suspended, and Retelet can get his poor paintings back. Finally, the Fleming becomes pink again: he is cleared! The guy sold thousands of fake Caesars without knowing anything about them: what a talent! The fakes were really exceptional!

LøL and I are appealing. We go back to court on March 28. The trial, planned to last three days, is completed in one afternoon, the judges and the prosecutor being *cooler*. Our strategy works. I get what I wanted - the return of the second part of my collection. I take the opportunity to take on myself what LøL was accused of, and his sentence is reduced by one year. What do the people want?

40. My new prison period [2010]

Not to lock himself in his crypt; to build new projects; to fight to recover his life and therefore his freedom: LøL and I are working on it. Between 2004 and his incarceration, he had already created *trashy* comics as well as skull sculptures because, according to him, death is the last taboo in our societies. I know that he often cried because he was forbidden to see Nello, his son.

In yet another example of blind administration, just before his release, the wardens searched LøL's cell. He was working on *Cortex Cape*, a board game for the whole family, in which players must escape from a maze where they are locked in. Upon discovering the elaborate plans that LøL has devised, the supervisors panic and transfer LøL to a maximum security ward for "planned escape"! He had to apply to the president of the court of appeal to be returned to his cell. Some time later, this game was published by a financier and was on sale everywhere!

For my part, I am alone in my cell at Les Baumettes. The director of the prison allows me to make drawings of "Caesar", chickens and centaurs, on paper that I yellow in my tea. I make about 300 of them under the amused and questioning gaze of the inmates and guards.

Having obtained all the necessary material, I also realize, in my cell where I am allowed to work, my own works. On basic materials, I create newspaper pages which were used as support for my collages covered with acrylic paint. As soon as possible, I will mount these pieces on canvas and stretcher, in order to express the horror of the detention and its cramped spaces. It is a pity that painting alone cannot completely translate the screams, the sounds, the noises of the inmates in panic and frustration. I bring out these fragile works on paper in rolls, via the families' visiting room. I want to make a personal exhibition of them as soon as I get out. In short, I recycle myself, rushing into my thoughts, personal analyses of my own work. Act of reinsertion, perhaps!

Of course, I signed up for the art workshops. I offer short drawing classes to other inmates who want to master charcoal, pencil and paint: for all of us, this forms a space of escape.

The catholic priest comes to the studio to ask me - who is rather atheist - to make large pieces on paper, so as to decorate the back of his improvised church in a bare and cold room as is the prison structure! I thank him and set to work to fulfill his order. He will be happy when, on the walls of his place of worship, we will hang these colorful works. This will earn me the honors of the inmates, the guards and the directors. I only tried to make this place more *fun!*

I am also anticipating my exit by ensuring the return of my personal collection. Once again authenticated, these pieces will soon be sold and bought by collectors. I still live on this sale.

41. My Piedoie period
[Since June 2011]

Since 2011, I've devoted myself to practicing my painting. It's more spiritually rewarding than making fakes, of course. On other levels, it is debatable. My knowledge of the market, of its mysteries, of its history, also allows me to broker modern and contemporary art, throughout the Art world. I sell Basquiat, Klein and Miró to billionaires all over the world. I also work with young artists who are developing their concept. Good luck to them, especially since some are already excellent forgers!

Being known on social networks and well referenced by Google for my trials, I thought that my antics would harm me. But no! Art is a dirty job, but someone has to do it! My fame, relative and unwanted, is a matter of acts mixed with truths, untruths and attitudes, all of which have been *blended in the mixer of life.* It is by this way that I found myself in the firmament of galleys and successes. The art world respects this.

We should live life in reverse. You start by dying, that eliminates that trauma that follows you all your life. Then you wake up in a nursing home, getting better every day. Then they kick you out under the pretext of good health and you start to get your pension. Then, on your first day of work, they give you a gold watch and you get a nice salary. You work for forty years until you are young enough to enjoy your working life. You go from party to party, you drink, you have lots of love affairs! You have no serious problems. You're getting ready to go to college. Then it's college, you have fun with your friends, without any obligation, and you end up becoming a baby. The last nine months are spent floating around, with central heating, *room service*, etc., and you leave this world in an orgasm!

All my life, I have chased the idea of having limits. This is what deceives people: they take my chances for skill and my mistakes for strategy. If the character I am known for annoys those who judge me from afar, those who approach me discover a boy who only wants to reach others through the heart. I know that my sweetest friendships come from this contrast. My legend keeps the fools away, intelligence suspects me. My solitude never seems really taciturn. I do not seek the light and show myself only at the hours of the great night parade.

Above all, I know that the artist is the reflection of all the beauty, all the darkness and all the decay of the world. The world must understand that art has a price and that the artist pays this price for all. Is it necessary to be gilded on edge to be adored? Is it necessary to do ten years in prison to be free? Do you have to do forty years of forgery to be real? I have created and made my dreams come true. I hope to offer to everyone, through this book, this small part of creation without which no man, artist or not, is ever quite human.

Contents

Contents 215